Affirm and Transform:
Affirmations for Self-Growth, Self-Knowing and Self-Loving

ANTOINETTE SPURRIER

Affirm and Transform:
Affirmations for Self-Growth, Self-Knowing and Self-Loving

Copyright © 2017 by Antoinette Spurrier

All rights reserved. No part of this book may be reproduced or transmitted in any form or by any means without written permission of the author.

ISBNs:
978-0-9971415-0-4 (paperback)
978-0-9856857-6-8 (hardback)
978-0-9856857-7-5 (eBook)

Printed in the United States of America

Dedication

This book is dedicated to:

Christian Francis

Connor Scott

Francisco Reynoso

David Scott

Each and every one of you has contributed generously to my life.

Contents

Introduction 1

I   The What and Why of Affirmations............. 5

II Our Dual Nature: The Limited Self
    and the Eternal Self 23

III Power-Charging Your Affirmations 57

IV Affirmations Change Consciousness............ 83

V   An Anthology of Spiritually-Based
    Affirmations 97

VI Thoughts for the Day: A Sampler............. 129

Acknowledgments

Collaborators

Jonathan Bewley,
photographer and media editor.

Andrew Freedman,
wordsmith who was the keeper of the intention; he expanded the book in scope, vitality and heart.

Jacqui Freedman,
artistic contributor who captures Spirit and Nature in her light-filled watercolors. Her work is available through Jacquifree@yahoo.com

Sherry (Heidi) Hall,
the woman with the velvet voice and empathetic heart, who gave inspirational input.

Jera Publishing
instrumental in bringing the Creating Deliberate Happiness series to completion.

Deborah Probst Kayes,
proofreader, coordinator, sustainer, and multi-tasker with extraordinary tenacity and patience.

Becky Lawton,
provider of multifaceted contributions.

Mark Murphy,
aka Mr. Creativity who provided graphic art input and inspiration.

Suresh Ramaswamy,
creative webmaster for FieldsOfLight.com

Anne Marie Welsh,
editor and dynamic catalyst for the birthing process of *Creating Deliberate Happiness: The Complete Guide* and this series.

AFFIRM AND TRANSFORM:

Special Mention

The Foundation for Personal and Spiritual Empowerment
FieldsOfLight.com

The San Diego Foundation

Yvonne Gorder Christenson for her artistic contributions.

My gratitude and appreciation also go to: Martin Anthony, Dr. James Ajemian, Rebecca and Todd Astill, Dr. Concepcion Barrio, The Bectold Family, Lou Bewersdorf, Wendell and Elaine Blonigan, Sheila Byrne, Renee and Sophia Carson, Cathi Eggleston, Joseph Escoffier, Susann and Richard Fishman, Christian Francis, Paul Gorsuch, Norma Grey, Kari Kashani, Nikki Mann, Sandra and Geoffrey Mavis, Deirdre Maher, Alvada and Weston Maughan, John McLaurin, Patrick and Catherine McNabb, Anne McQuillan, Kevin McQuillen, Ron and Marlane Miriello, Ken and Betsy Mullen, Dr. Carl and Chris Murphy, Chaitanya Narayan, Jim and Kathleen Newcomb, Brian and Emily Quinn, Francisco Reynoso, Ginger Palmer, Jan Saucier, Connor Scott, Judy Segal, Jeffrey Spurrier, David and Rose Spurrier, Ann Summa, Lisa Baker Scurr & Ron Scurr, Ricardo Torres-Roldan and Family, Penny Wing, and Victor Nacif.

In Memoriam

John Laurence,
teacher, mentor and spiritual advisor. He was blessed with spiritual gifts that he shared unselfishly with others. He was instrumental in who I have become.

John McLaurin,
who personified friendship and sustained constancy, loyalty and love in that friendship. We journeyed together in the past and will do so again.

Linda Provence Diehl,
a beloved friend who expressed in wonderful ways both analytical thought and intuitive knowing. She made everyone feel that she had the ability to be mother to all.

Charles Mirandon,
who contributed through his friendship and loving support of our family and projects for decades.

BRIDGE WITH STREAM

Yvonne G. Christenson

Introduction

To the Reader,

Affirm and Transform: Affirmations for Self-Growth, Self-Knowing and Self-Loving is the fourth installment in my series that culminated in *Creating Deliberate Happiness: The Complete Guide*. This shorter work distills key themes from that larger book, and it presents practical exercises to ignite the power of spiritualized affirmations to change your habits of consciousness and by doing so, change your life.

I warmly invite you to explore your own habits of thought, and then, with introspection and practice, to bring about fundamental changes in your ways of thinking. These changes in consciousness will allow you to charge your affirmations with conviction and, in time, to manifest the blessings you deserve in your life and work. When properly applied, affirmations and meditation can lead to personal and spiritual empowerment, to powerful transformation and growth.

This book on the power of affirmations is not meant to replace the larger book. The full *Deliberate Happiness* analyzes the background to these practices and explains the natural patterns and scientific laws governing emotional and spiritual growth. Here I focus on a sequence of techniques and ideas that, with patience and persistence, will bring the transformation you desire. The techniques include:

- Spiritual practices of meditation, visualizations, journaling, introspection and especially, affirmations.

Affirm and Transform:

- Ways of confronting deservedness issues by uprooting negative self-talk and altering any feelings of worthlessness that sabotage love and happiness.

- A realistic focus on how aligning your Limited and Eternal Selves and practicing affirmations will overcome negative thoughts and behaviors that can result when you seek to make lasting change.

My intention is to assist you in claiming your highest and best self. As you better understand spiritual law and these techniques, you will eventually return to your natural state of happiness, on the path to joy.

Antoinette Spurrier

San Diego, California

ANGELS WITH BELLS

Yvonne G. Christenson

CHAPTER ONE

The What and Why of Affirmations

Properly understood and applied, spiritualized affirmations assist us in personal and spiritual empowerment and transformation. By affirming ideas that reflect spiritual truth, we align with that truth and deepen our self-knowing. This helps us manifest greater happiness.

KEY TOPICS ADDRESSED IN THIS CHAPTER:
- Defining affirmations.
- Discovering whether affirmations are for you.
- Journaling, and journaling exercises for greater self-knowledge.
- Practicing meditation and affirmations, a powerful duo.
- Learning how to meditate.
- Practicing effective affirmations.

AFFIRMATIONS DEFINED

In every day speech, you may use the word "affirm" simply to denote "yes" or a larger positive assertion of your ideas or your self. Affirmation as used here, however, applies to a specific technique, based on spiritual and scientific principles, that creates a heightened level of alignment of your consciousness with Spirit. This alignment will allow you to tap into the very force of creation and claim more of your true nature as a spiritual being. By stating an affirmation, you claim your nature in words and then these energized words penetrate and expand into deeper recesses of self-knowledge. Affirmations used properly have the power to activate your spiritual potency. Through the faithful and correct practice of affirmations, you may align yourself to the truth of your own spiritual nature.

This can happen because the words of an affirmation create a spiritualized force field with energy, movement and momentum. Affirmations thus start a potent vibration, which corresponds to both an energy frequency and a state of consciousness in seed form. Affirmations become power charged by your focused attention and will-based energy. Energized repetition is Key.

Over time, the affirmation begins to override smaller vibrations, even negative thoughts, and those eventually become absorbed by the affirmative statement.

KEY GENERAL CONCEPTS ABOUT AFFIRMATIONS

Affirmations are effective if you want to:

- Change negative circumstances in your life to positive.
- Unleash your creative power.
- Create new possibilities in your life.
- Explore new talents and new dimensions of yourself.
- Heighten your powers of imagination and visualization.
- Stop negative self-talk and uproot tenacious negative thoughts.
- Deepen spiritual life by exploring and expanding consciousness.

The What and Why of Affirmations

Change Your Thoughts, Change Your Life

As we change our thoughts, we change our energy. As we change our energy, that which is attracted to us changes.

Spiritual law truly operates in that way. No matter what your conditions, you have the power to redefine them. No matter what your situation, you have the power to visualize something different and something new. No matter what your circumstances, your power to co-create with the universe is amplified by your participation with it. Your nature, as energized love and light, is in search of its own highest vibration.

Affirmations are a true and valid tool of transformation. Their power resides not only in the capacity to positively impact the Limited Self, that part of yourself existing in a material world subject to decay and death; affirmations also lead to greater self-integration. They can create a bridge between your diverging selves—Limited and Eternal—thus promoting alignment, attunement, and harmonious cooperation between them.

To understand any resistance you may encounter, you first must understand your own dual nature as both a Limited Self and an Eternal Self. As you will learn further in Chapter Two, these selves are in frequent communication and yet function in

> *The brain is made up of tiny nerve cells called 'neurons'. These neurons have tiny branches that reach out and connect to other neurons to form a neural net. Each place where they connect is incubated into a thought or a memory. Now, the brain builds up all its concepts by the law of associative memory. For example, ideas, thoughts and feelings are all constructed and interconnected in this neural net and all have a possible relationship with one another.*
> FROM THE MOVIE
> *What the Bleep Do We Know?*

nearly opposite ways. This is not an abstract philosophical quandary; it is a reality. The Limited Self is identified and bound by your physical form, mind, feelings and culture. The other, the Eternal Self, expresses your spiritual nature, your true unchangeable essence.

Affirmations alter energy and thought patterns because your habitual attitudes form neural circuits in the brain. By choosing different habitual thoughts, you rewire the brain, creating new pathways to form new attitudes about yourself and/or your relationships.

Donald Olding Hebb, the father of neuropsychology and author of *The Organization of Behavior*, wrote extensively on the function of neurons, or nerve cells, and how they contribute to psychological processes. His theory is often summarized as *"cells that fire together, wire together."* This firing and wiring takes place in the synapses between neurons where information (communication) is transferred. The latest research indicates that memories and beliefs are stored in the neurons.

Effective affirmations from your conscious mind can and do reprogram (re-wire) your non-conscious or subconscious mind. Over time, you will find that affirmations, combined with imagination, can change your faulty self-definitions. Affirmations can free up energy to conceive and define yourself in new and life-enhancing ways that will help you align your two selves. This unleashes tremendous power, a power that can then naturally influence your life, your creativity, and your relationships with others.

How Can Affirmations Change and Transform Your Life?

Affirmations are a technique for the transformation of consciousness. When practiced with focused, energized concentration and a systematic technique, the repetition of spiritual truth stirs the consciousness to remembrance and issues a sacred invitation to awake to who you truly are—for all of us are divinity reflecting in the journey of matter. Affirmations, energized with commitment, can:

1. Change your mental habits of negativity to positive claiming.
2. Change your habits of emotional reactivity. We create habits of by associating emotions with events. The repetition of associated ideas and feelings ingrains habits of reaction.
3. Change habits of thinking around worthiness and deservedness. Habits and feeling states around a lack of deservedness can damage every vital area of life.
4. Integrate diverging aspects of the finite self, here referred to as the Limited Self. Systematic use of affirmations power charges your life; they are tools of transformation and change.
5. Open your mind and heart to accept and embrace the sacred invitations life offers. (The next chapter delves more deeply into the concept of sacred invitations.)

Journaling To Discover Who You Truly Are

When we approach journaling with an open mind and heart, and we commit to being completely candid with ourselves, we open up to limitless opportunity for growth and healing. Through total honesty, we begin to peel away the layers of our psyche. The masks we wear begin to fall away, revealing our true nature – who we are when we aren't "the parent, the employee, the friend" and are just ourselves.

CHRISTIN SYNDER, *The Healing Power of Journaling*

A helpful step toward effective affirmations and a key tool in the transformation of consciousness, journaling can help unlock your mind and open your heart. When you reveal yourself more fully to yourself, you can then affirm ideas that will truly place you on the road to happiness and joy. Journaling allows you to focus on your habits in consciousness and to identify the areas we need to change. By understanding yourself better through journaling, you can proceed with depth and clarity.

The habit of journaling not only leads to greater awareness of yourself, but can create a journey map that, in the end, leads to self-discovery. Journaling honestly, deeply and regularly can both clarify ideas and open fresh windows of introspection. Asking tough questions and writing down answers may allow you to go deeper into self-understanding instead of remaining at a surface level of awareness about yourself.

If you are to use spiritualized affirmations to create a more happy and abundant life and become a more effective co-creator with the universe, then you will need to explore your personal perspective on the subject of happiness. Journaling is a way to see those attitudes, expectations, and feelings about happiness. By writing an inventory of your present state of happiness, you can create a baseline to assess your growth. You can see your own capacity to achieve the state of mind that might lead you to achieve enduring happiness.

You are invited to do these journal exercises in the spirit of self-discovery. You may be in a state of perfect health, and have abundant opportunities and meaningful relationships, but you may still feel unhappy or dissatisfied. You may also see happiness as a future goal, unattainable in the present. Danger lurks in always thinking "I will be happy later." That becomes an affirmation in which you are telling yourself, "Don't be happy now. You can't be happy now. Be happy later." Such ideas poison the Now. The Now is all you have and all you will ever have in life, if only you —and all of us—knew it.

Journaling Activity: Are You Happy Now?

Write down your present feelings about being emotionally fulfilled and possessing inner contentment.

- Is your daily frame of mind peaceful and joy-filled?

- How much is your happiness tied to the past?
- How much is tied to the future?
- How much is tied to career?
- How much to expectations around others?
- Is happiness in your life on the installment plan?

If you answered yes to the last two questions, you might ask yourself how many years do you believe it will take for a desired accomplishment to happen? Do you assume that contentment, inner satisfaction, and happiness will be the result?

Finally, you might ask whether whatever you desire or want to acquire any way violates the wellbeing or the happiness of another.

Penetrate into the Stillness: A Short Course on Meditation

If the doors of perception were cleansed, everything would appear to us as it is, Infinite.

WILLIAM BLAKE

Meditation is another crucial technique that will assist you in power charging your affirmation practice. In fact, even more than journaling, meditation is fundamental to any deep changes in consciousness, and to any life change. By meditating, all people — no matter how fearful, violent or lost—can open themselves to the sacred within and become free. Meditation allows us access to the deeper regions of our spiritual nature, connects us with the Divine presence within, and provides us a clearer vision of the truth. Positive affirmations are truth uttered in sound.

Scheduling time each day for meditation practice is essential not only for peace and well-being, but for discovering the Self. Interiorized consciousness opens you to your spiritual nature. Together, meditation and journaling strengthen will-based affirmations and can lead toward the experience of the Eternal Self, your true source of lasting happiness. (See Chapter Two for more on integrating our dual nature, the Limited Self and the Eternal Self.) I suggest, however, that you should continue your practice of affirmations even while you attempt to master the arts of journaling and meditation, even as you gradually understand how to integrate your dual nature as described in the next chapter. You need to chisel your way toward forming new thoughts in order to reveal the masterpiece of who you truly are. The key to maximizing progress with affirmations is to commit to the path to success in the beginning. This poem describes that journey:

Leap-Frogging Mind

Mind, Mind
Splintering, leaping mind
Unite with the breath
Of being.

Mind, Mind
Leap frogging player
Plumb the depths of
Your cavern of Knowing.

Mind, Mind
Dissolve your restless frenzy.
The net of peace
Shall catch you
Tenderly.

Mind, Mind
Go beyond that Lily pad
Of distraction.
Serenity beacons, joy awaits.

Mind, Mind
Consciousness supreme,
The net of peace
Shall catch you
Tenderly.

There are countless meditation techniques available and myriad philosophies about the proper method of meditation. Finding an effective and suitable style of meditation may take time, but will prove invaluable.

Note: Highly effective, balanced meditation techniques are available from Self-Realization Fellowship in the form of lessons delivered to your home every two weeks. Contact:

Self-Realization Fellowship
3880 San Rafael Drive
Los Angeles, CA 90065-3219
323-225-2471
http//www.yogananda-srf.org

One technique that will bring consistent results is offered below. This technique has some similarities to a Self-Realization Fellowship method, but is not connected with or based on the work of that organization.

Meditation Technique

The proper posture for meditation is very important.

- Sit comfortably on a straight back chair.
- Place the feet on the floor or a flat surface, pointed straight ahead.
- Maintain a straight spine, yet without strain or discomfort.
- Place your hands, with palms turned gently up, near the crease between your hips and thighs, or slightly lower on the upper thighs.
- Note: Meditation techniques, in general, should not be practiced in a position where the individual is lying down in a bed. When lying down, the meditative state too easily becomes a sleep state. If an individual has the physical ability to sit either in a chair with feet flat on the floor—or cross-legged on the floor on a flat surface—the sitting posture should be assumed. In general, avoid sitting on a bed, for consciousness usually associates the bed with sleep.

This meditation technique involves focusing your attention at the point between the eyebrows known as the "third eye" or spiritual eye. This is a center that increases our spiritual connectedness as we focus upon it. If you are having difficulty in achieving or maintaining the proper eye position for your meditation, the following suggestion may assist you in getting the correct angle for your focus gaze. The eyes should be turned gently and slightly upward.

The What and Why of Affirmations

Pencil Technique for Proper Gaze

Visualize holding a #2 pencil eraser at the spiritual eye. Visualize the eraser resting on the forehead between and slightly above the eyebrows, centered at the spiritual eye. The pencil should be parallel to the floor. Allow your focus to move to where you visualize the point of the pencil to be. Keep the gaze focused at that spot. This technique is not part of the practice itself, but is a tool that will prevent you from placing excessive strain on the eyes and help develop a better habit pattern for meditation.

Note: There should be no strain or tension. This is a natural, pleasant position for the eyes.

Preparation for Meditation:

- Visualize that you are encircled by white light that either outlines the body or is shaped as a spherical egg-shape. It is the <u>intention</u> to place white light around the body that summons a greater connection with Spirit and strengthens the energy field.

- After visualizing the white light in this way, begin to observe the breath in a relaxed state of mind. Maintain the correct posture with spine erect and feet flat on the floor.

- Affirm that you are divinely protected by the surrounding white light of Spirit. (Example: "I am surrounded by the light field of the Divine. I am ever protected. I am ever embraced by the Divine Force.") Repeat this protection affirmation, or a similar one, between 12-16 times.

- Now, in this relaxed state of mind, begin to observe the breath without any attempt to regulate it. Neither speed up nor slow down the rhythm of the breath. Simply observe the inhalation and exhalation as it naturally flows in and out.

- See yourself as "piggy-backing" on each inhalation and exhalation. Mentally say, "I ride the inward breath." As you naturally begin to exhale, mentally say "I ride the outward breath." Continue this pattern for approximately 15 minutes. Visualize yourself riding the inward breath and the outward breath. Then change the repetition of words on the inhaling and exhaling breath to "I am That".

Additional affirmations may be mentally repeated prior to or following the use of this meditation technique:

> *I ride the inward breath.*
> *I ride the outward breath.*
> *I am one with that breath.*
> *Reveal Thyself.*

You will accelerate your ability to find stillness if, for three weeks, you practice meditation, journaling and these other components of your ritual of transformation every day.

- **Meditating for a minimum of 10 minutes.**
- **Journaling for 15 minutes on this theme.**
- **Positive introspection.**
- **Holding a Thought for the Day.**
- **Repeating One or More Affirmations.**

Your thought for the day will likely be a simple truth such as this one from Mother Theresa, "If you judge people, you have no time to love them." Or perhaps it will be a more complex thought such as this one from the great Irish poet, W. B. Yeats: "We can make our minds so like still water that beings gather about us that they may see, it may be, their own images and so live for a moment with a clearer, perhaps even with a fiercer life because of our quiet."

Or you may wish to ponder a poem on the theme of stillness and tranquility. Here is a good one by Wendell Berry:

Go Among Trees and Sit Still

> I go among trees and sit still.
> All my stirring becomes quiet
> Around me like circles on water.
> My tasks lie in their places
> Where I left them, asleep like cattle.
> Then what I am afraid of comes.
> I live for a while in its sight.
> What I fear in it leaves it,
> And the fear of it leaves me.
> It sings, and I hear its song.

Many other thoughts for the day are included in the final section of the book, Chapter Six.

During the meditation portion of your practice, you may also choose an affirmation to begin the practice or to intensify your focus with a spiritually centered thought. Repeat it over mentally five or six times to help you maintain focus. Here are two possibilities:

> *I mount*
> *the incoming breath.*
> *I ride to the end.*
> *I let the breath*
> *begin its descent*
> *while I mount for the*
> *downward ride.*
> *I ride the breath*
> *of mind.*

Affirm and Transform:

Or

*Still lake of peace,
I drink tranquility.
I sip waters of knowing.
I penetrate the stillness.*

However, while you may begin the meditation practice by the repetition of affirmations, do not continue while in the interiorized meditative state itself. The restless mind is always attempting to re-energize the meditator. To bring the affirmations again to a state of calm interiorized consciousness can re-engage the leap frogging mind, at that point, and disrupt the depth being achieved.

My Name was the Name of All

I affirm my essence.
I affirm my being.
My words spoke the truth of who I am.

I am that essence.
I am that creator.
I am that being.

I affirm my essence.
I affirm my being.
My name is the name of All.

As I called my name
My essence emerged
Into powerful form
From the field of light.

As I called my name
I beheld the truth:
The field of light
was my own.

A Daily Ritual or Sadhana

If meditation is already a part of your daily practice or, once it has become comfortable for you, it is wise to continue practicing all the elements that can bring you closer and deeper into your true self, your spiritual consciousness. Repetition accelerates foundational change, establishing new patterns of thought that other activities such as reading cannot create. By revolving new positive thoughts in your mind, you will create new energy grooves in your brain. As noted above, during this process of reprogramming, your day should include:

- **meditating for ten minutes or more.**
- **journaling for fifteen minutes.**
- **a thought for the day.**
- **a spiritualized affirmation.**

Write your chosen affirmation on five, 3x5 file cards. Place those cards over your desk, on your bathroom mirror, above the kitchen sink, on your car dashboard—where ever you are most likely to see the card and thus be reminded to say the affirmation again. You may speak it out loud or mentally, depending upon circumstances. Aim for fifteen repetitions each day. This daily practice should become the heart of your effort to systematically begin to create change.

UTAH NATIONAL PARK
Myrtle Gorder

CHAPTER TWO

OUR DUAL NATURE: THE LIMITED SELF AND THE ETERNAL SELF

Whether you are aware of it or not, your silent, spiritual Self beckons you. Your desire for happiness is a response to a distant trumpet call summoning you homeward to Spirit.

KEY TOPICS ADDRESSED IN THIS CHAPTER ARE:
- Why we pursue happiness.
- Introduction and exploration of the Limited Self.
- Introduction and exploration of the Eternal Self.
- The conflict between these two selves.
- Limited Self's pursuit of happiness.
- Eternal Self's natural state of happiness and joy.
- Self-knowing tied to your spiritual journey.
- Reframing experiences to awake your inner knowing.

- Meditation, visualization and affirmations to bridge the selves.
- Sacred invitations: learning to accept and embrace them.
- Integration of the Limited and Eternal Selves.
- Affirmations for integration.

The Essence of Happiness

The subject of happiness is so profound that it is written about in the world's great literature as well as in its eminent spiritual traditions. The pursuit of happiness is a fundamental right, referenced in the U.S. Constitution. It is a driving force that underlies our ventures and adventures in this physical world. Happiness also can be intensely consuming and powerful in and of itself.

But why do we pursue happiness? Is it simply a reflex effort to avoid pain, or is it a distinct drive to access a greater, higher state of pleasure? Is pleasure simply experienced at the physical and psychological levels, or could there be a state of transcendent pleasure that is tied to our spiritual nature? With a need so basic, so deeply intrinsic to our nature, why does happiness remain elusive?

Without understanding your dual nature, human and divine, your efforts to "find" happiness are misplaced. Happiness on the material level is transitory—a vanishing specter of possibility. The more you and others experience our true natures, however, the greater the experience of self-empowerment and then joy, our native state.

Our dilemma is that we have two opposing selves, in frequent communication and yet functioning in nearly opposite ways. This is not an abstract philosophical quandary; it is a pervasive reality. Our lack of conscious awareness of these two selves complicates our attempts to achieve peace, harmony, and happiness. Mankind's deepest expressions of philosophical and religious thought refer to this internal schism. Present-day author and psychologist John Welwood puts it succinctly: "To discover our human wholeness…we need to bring the two sides of our nature— absolute and relative, supra-personal and personal, heaven and earth—together at last." This integration offers hope for healing the schism and finding inner peace and happiness.

The Two Selves Defined

It is helpful to discover what is true by distinguishing it from what is not true. The clearer your perceptions, the greater your ability to discern subtle nuances of illusion. For this reason, please join me in taking a deeper look at these two selves and how they operate in polarized consciousness. One, for the sake of this discussion, will be called the Limited Self, identified and bound by the physical form, mind, feelings and the culture in which it lives. The other, the Eternal Self, expresses your spiritual nature, our true unchangeable essence.

> *Awakening is when the eyes of consciousness open so that consciousness begins to see what is real, instead of consciousness seeing only an illusion, or what it wants to be real.*
>
> JOHN DE RUITER
> *Dialogues with Emerging Spiritual Teachers*

Put simply, the Limited Self consists of:

- Your chemical, biological nature, operating in the physical dimension under physiological laws.

- Your psychological layers of mental consciousness, operating within a social context.

- Your beliefs and life experiences, operating within your environment and culture.

- Your extraordinary ability to evaluate, interpret and assign meaning to your experiences, literally defining yourself through your imagination.

Because you may never have viewed the interface between these four aspects, your Limited Self may feel compartmentalized, incorrectly

> *The inner battle is between our lower self, or pseudo-self—the body identified ego—and our true higher self, the soul, the image of God within us.*
>
> PARAMAHANSA YOGANANDA

interpreting experiences and events, wrongly imagining yourself as a body identified, continuously changing, impermanent being.

Even if the Limited Self is unaware of its spiritual potential, it nonetheless carries the capacity for joy within. However, fragmentation, conflict, and persistent habits of thought—including the habit of worry, circular negative thinking and defeating self-talk—become major impediments on the road to happiness and self-awareness.

Your other self, the expansive Eternal Self, is your true spiritual nature, pursuing nothing, for its state of consciousness is joy transcendent. That Self, your soul nature, is always aware of the actions and activities of the Limited Self. This spiritual essence manifests in subtle, powerful ways as the expression of who you truly are.

All physical life contains the movement of Divine Intelligence through the vibratory law of creation. As a human being, you have an innate capacity to unfold through developmental stages into a multi-faceted being with highly advanced, complex thoughts, a vivid imagination, sparks of divine creativity and the ability to plan and achieve goals. Part of the miracle of your life is that your magnificence in this form will never come again in exactly the same place, in the same way. Each of us is unique in the Universe. *Your* individual expression is unlike anyone else's.

Unfortunately, we generally go about life unaware of our infinite potential, for we are focused primarily on three-dimensional reality. We access knowledge through our bio-chemical nature and filter experiences through the individual persona, or ego. The five senses, as necessary as they are in helping us navigate this physical dimension, are like a twelve-inch ruler. They can measure the "fiber and texture" of the material world, but they cannot reach or measure Infinity.

Relentless forces of change assault this Limited Self, for nothing stays the same in this world. Even the semi-permanent values and mores of the society are in a constant state of flux. As the world spins around you in an ever-changing panorama of experiences, your life is impacted in ways great and small. Events happen, and you interpret and assign meaning to them. This capacity adds both to the wonder and the complexity to life. More often than not, however, you probably interpret events subjectively rather than objectively. If you are like most of us humans, you place a fog—a kind of conceptual overlay—onto your experiences and then make an emotional investment in that overlay, taking it to be "real" in and of itself.

But you also have an innate ability to reflect on yourself, a trait that lends resilience to your nature. Your ability to interpret and imagine can open a door to new interpretations and redefinitions. You can restructure the meaning you see in the physical dimension. "Consciousness is imaginative, sensitive and pliable; it can think and dream itself into any state," wrote Indian scholar and sage, Paramahansa Yogananda. He is referring here to your amazing ability to re-create ourselves, to change and transform consciousness itself.

While the capacity for self-motivated change is always present, the Limited Self is more often changed by biological or psychological conditions that continually impact it. It is altered by the hands of circumstances and the clay of environment: childhood and our early upbringing, genetics, and diet are just a few of the influences that continually impact this Limited Self. With such a constant bombardment, where there is really no telling what may happen in the next moment, is there any wonder the Limited Self feels powerlessness against the law of change?

Affirm and Transform:

Stranger O' Self

Stranger o' Self
Dream Self gone wandering
Among the ruins of time
Gone to find self meeting self
Yet strangers always.

Stranger o' Self
Viewed from countless mirrors
Reflectors of false images
Self seeing self
Distorted on a mirror of glass.

Unknown substance
in search of form.
Stranger, Dream Self
Gone wandering
Among the ruins of time.

To operate entirely from the Limited Self makes the pursuit of happiness a precarious journey. "The only constant, is change," wrote the Greek philosopher Heraclitus. You do indeed live largely in a world of unending change over which none of us has true control.

But even in assessing yourself through this limited, changeable self, you can continue to define and interpret. This is a deeply significant truth that will be reinforced throughout this book. In my counseling work through the years, I have seen clients—once awakened to their intrinsic capacity—choose new perspectives, come to reframe even the most difficult memories and experiences.

By Reframing Your Experience, You Will Awaken Your Inner Knowing

To awaken your inner knowing is to discover another, truer part of yourself that often is not experienced but awaits discovery. That discovery can liberate you, for it holds the promise of inner contentment, joy, and self-knowledge. Nothing has ever occurred to you that did not involve some level of your own participation. Even if you are not the initiator of specific actions, you participate in that which you experience. You may have lacked power over certain events or actions, but no matter what has been taken away from us, if you empower your mind and imagination, you still have the power to interpret events. Your mind, thoughts, and perceptions define and explain your experiences. Mind is the definer and the interpreter, as well as the creator. Your power to interpret, mentally redefine, and reframe your life experiences is a powerful tool of freedom and new creation. When you imagine, you sow the seeds of creation. As you charge energized belief with spiritualized affirmations, you deepen the energy of possible creation. Repetition of those affirmations charges these ideas and with energized, will-based mental activity, so that you can create the new.

What if Tragic Circumstances Affect Your Peaceful Self-Knowing?

Even your worst experiences, which you were powerless to prevent, can be reframed in your consciousness by exploring possible avenues of service to others. If you have been in a place of true suffering, nothing will change that experience. But the desire to expand that knowledge of suffering can build a new bridge to others over which your compassion walks. It is a bridge by which others may benefit and a bridge of freedom for you if you feel trapped and powerless over your circumstances. When your feet lack the power to walk to a new way of doing things, trust that the heart has the capacity to grow wings.

Affirm and Transform:

What you viewed negatively as a traumatic event can be redefined in your mind and imagination, then empowered by your affirmations as an opportunity. Tragic circumstances may sow the seeds of your creative power, which then blossoms to help yourself and others.

Because you possess consciousness, you possess the power to create, recreate, frame and reframe any and all experiences. No one can take away from you your own imagination. You always possess the power to align with the Source of all creation. Your imagination creates your masterpiece by the act of mental imaging. Together, your consciousness and being form a unified expression of Spirit. You are immutable, unchangeable, and enduring. In the process of awakening this inner knowing, your journey of consciousness may take you into the domain and absolute power of Spirit. You are a diamond light reflection of that Spirit. This discovery awaits you now. Believe you are prepared to make the journey now. You are the discovery itself.

One deterrent to making this discovery and achieving deep happiness may be your self-assessment around the subject of your deservedness. Negative thoughts and feelings may tell you that you do not deserve to be in a place of receiving, discovering and inner-knowing or that you lack the ability to materialize good in your life. These ideas and feelings can merge in powerful mental constructs and energy grooves that inhibit or limit your access to the universal stream of possibilities. When the energy from the Creative Source that created everything and everyone is allowed to flow in your life, you become divinely infused with that energy of all creation. This stream of energy is not separate from the Spiritual Source; it is the Spiritual Source manifesting itself in you. You are an individualized expression of that Spiritual Source.

Now for the questions:

- How do you align with that Spiritual Source?
- How do you see your own nature – as primarily biological or primarily spiritual?

Our Dual Nature: The Limited Self and the Eternal Self

- Are there ways or means by which you may become more aware of that Source?
- Can you create a greater attunement to that Source itself?
- Is it possible for you to become a better co-producer in the drama of creation and manifestation?
- Do you feel separate and alone, unable to access the Source that created us?
- Do you doubt that there is an Eternal Source from which we all spring?
- Or do you already see yourself as part of that Divine Source on a journey to discover more of your self, your nature, and your true being?

You cannot and should not wait until you feel fully deserving before you act. The universe is a container of both positive and negative forces. You also are a container in which both positive and negative energies are expressed according to actual laws of attraction and repulsion. Negative energy in the universe may tell you that you are not ready to move forward. Those inner statements and feelings of self-doubt may come as whispers of negation. But those whispers contain the negative force of the universe itself, in direct repulsion against the light. They may come as whispers in your ear, but the power and the energy of that negativity resounds into the universe itself. Sometimes you may doubt that there is a divine light or spiritual energy with love as its essence. If you persevere with intention, you will prove over time the truth of your spiritual existence. You will affirm, with great clarity and internal perception, your connectedness to the light and to all creation. If you go forward, acting as if it is so, even if you do not feel it or believe it yet, you shall begin to see the truth of that testimony of the light.

Affirm and Transform:

Spiritually-Based Affirmations As A Tool to Uproot and Eliminate Deservedness Issues

By systematic repetition of truth contained in Spirit, you may claim your inherent ability to co-create with the Divine. You should not underestimate the power of energized, spiritually-based affirmations in bringing a flow of positive energy into your life. Dynamic intention fused with affirmations creates an energized flow. Will-based affirmations access the power and energy of the force field of creation. Successful people use that principle when they create and experience their own lives. You may also employ that same principle to realize your potential and achieve more success in your inner and outer lives.

Until you claim that power to choose, reframe and affirm, and until that choosing comes from your more enlightened, expanded Eternal Self, your perceptions will be constrained by the Limited Self's view of reality. What you see, hear, sense, feel and therefore experience, is filtered through the mind with all its pre-conditioning. You probably believe your thoughts and perceptions are real, regardless of their origin. Roger Walse, in his "State of the Integral Enterprise: Part 1," wrote: "What is crucial to recognize is that all perceptions reflect perspectives, and all perspectives are partial and selective. Each perspective both reveals and conceals, clarifies and distorts. However, perspectives and perceptions do not clearly reveal their own limitations."

Assumptions and perceptions can harden into beliefs, which can manifest, consciously or unconsciously, as behaviors. It is imperative, therefore, that you learn to recognize how this process of self- definition operates.

As long as limiting beliefs remain unknown and unconscious, you remain a puppet, pulled on the strings of conditioned behaviors or false concepts of yourself. As a result, you will continue to experience a limited range of happiness. Fortunately, at your best, you will naturally strive for the experience of knowing yourself as integrated and whole.

Personality is Ego-driven

Your personality, as delightful and creative as it may be, is limited to the perceptions of mind and body alone. Its drives are primarily based on preservation, survival, the elimination of pain, finding pleasure, and satisfying the senses, none of which, as we have seen, can provide true happiness. Nature intended for the ego-based personality to survive, reproduce, and endure. The emphasis of this ego-based personality is thus always upon the "I," which has little capacity to extend beyond itself to the needs, the necessities, the wants and desires of others.

Human experience creates a kind of hypnosis in which we identify with the Limited Self. Jean Paul Sartre, the French existentialist, wrote: "Everything happens as if consciousness were hypnotized by this ego which it has established, which it has constructed, becoming absorbed in it as if to make the ego its guardian and law."

With this myopic view, the ego rarely sees beyond itself. Generally, the activities and drives of this ego-based personality do not allow for the stillness in which we can hear the call of the vastly subtler self. That other self, your soul nature, is ever in residence even as you live in your physical-material reality. This self is hidden by the noise and drives of the world and a lack of attention to its existence.

Your Developmental Stages

Your entry into the material world as an infant was driven foremost by the biology of survival. It is hardly a journey of mystical contemplation! From this beginning, the infant is on a journey of growing and expressing increased mastery of its biology. The developmental progression from birth at a physical and psychological level has definite patterns and transitions. Certain milestones of development that are age specific must occur if there is to be a normal physical and psychological growth and maturation.

Renowned psychoanalyst Erik Erikson addressed specifically the developmental stages and the areas of attempted psychological mastery that must occur in those specific stages. Piaget's classic work on children also shows us stages of child development using copious research, observation, and journey metaphors; he reveals this development through the eyes of the child, providing a clear view of the Limited Self's dominance in young human consciousness.

If a child grows with the proper guidance, developmental stages occur in proper sequence. These stages, however, are influenced by the interaction of parents, significant others, and the community in which the child lives. Through words, example and behaviors powerful messages are delivered to the child: these contribute to his own self-identification. The child receives both overt and covert messages; these have enormous potential for interpretation, adding to the intrigue and complexity of the youth's emotional and psychological journey.

> *What really has to (go) is our false self created by our own mind, ego, and culture. It is a pretense, a bogus identity, a passing fad, a psychological construct that gets in the way of who we are and always were.... This is the objective and metaphysical True Self.*
>
> RICHARD ROHR

The Limited Self is naturally rooted in this journey. Being human involves the physiological wiring of our nature in a physical world. By necessity, the child focuses on gaining greater skill over specific needs, mastering the body, and navigating physically in the world. This leads to body-based self-identification.

No wonder our self-esteem is reinforced by the idea that external mastery in the physical world is a natural source of happiness! So many messages in society reinforce this. Athletes become heroes; fashion models are idolized. Popularity is often based on glamour, wealth, and personality. Is it any wonder the young psyche can become confused?

The absorption and interpretation of messages, impressions and ideas create an experience of self-identity. There are not only layers upon layers of experience, but enmeshed layers of subtle reinforcement. The co-mingling of these layers create the masquerade of the "real self."

With the increasing capacity to contemplate, examine and verbalize experiences, the child feels that what we are calling the Limited Self is actually the core reality of his essence. Since the Limited Self must, of necessity, be identified with its biological journey in the physical, material world, it strives to access the world from this early core identification. The child seeks its happiness from the senses and the material world. Although the progressive formation of this Limited Self results in an undeniably real self, we are, in truth, something vastly more complex, more wondrous.

Though most individuals abandon the ideas and desires of youth by changing or modifying them with experience, most still claim this Limited Self as solid and enduring even though the frailty of that perception can be seen in the reflecting mirror of changing experiences. One of the great delusive ideas posits the solidity and permanence of the Limited Self amidst impermanence and fragmentation.

The more you are able to bring these distorted, fragmented areas to conscious awareness, the greater will be the possibility of integrating them. The greater the denial about opposing parts within yourself, the greater the potential that there will be conflict and a lack of personal integration. Denial and lack of self-knowledge

> *The ego feeling we are aware of now is…only a shrunken vestige of a far more extensive feeling – a feeling which embraced the universe and expressed an inseparable connection of the ego with the external world.*
>
> SIGMUND FREUD

perpetuate fragmentation and lessen your chances of experiencing continuous fulfillment and happiness.

Illusory Happiness

When asked to write down what we feel would give us happiness, many of us will naturally respond with answers centered on physical-material objects, or success in that realm. Some responses will be relationship-based or about love and happiness, generally. Often we believe that the possession of, or the constant access to another person is the source of our happiness. This is because the Limited Self does not fully understand that the desire to experience love is also an invitation to know more of the Eternal Self. Instead, it interprets love as a sensory or material experience associated with its own nature.

Happiness for the Limited Self has to be, in some way, tied to the experiences or desires of life in a physical body in a material world. In this state of being, our capacity for happiness is not only determined by our habitual state of mind, whether positive or negative, but by our emotional response to events. Emotions become charged with expectation and interpretation. This generally leads to replaying and reinterpreting along similar ideas or themes. Memory replay is again subject to interpretation. And off we go on a repetitive cycle that is difficult to break. Let's take a deeper look at how thought patterns work.

How Habit Patterns are Formed

Our interpretations of events create energy. This blueprint energy creates grooves in our brains that allow for further movement of energy through which our consciousness travels. New experiences tend to gravitate into existing energy grooves. Once a particular thought groove is activated by a repetitive thought, a tendency is formed. It is extremely difficult to change the tendencies of the physical mind for so many of our thoughts are automatic and therefore unconscious.

In the last few decades, scientists have shown that we can change the structure and function of our brains by the way we think. This newly conceptualized feature of the brain is called neuroplasticity. For years, the conventional wisdom of neuroscience held that the hardware of the brain is fixed and immutable – that we are stuck with what we were born with. Yet *Wall Street Journal* science writer, Sharon Begley, reveals an entirely new paradigm in her book, *Train the Mind, Change the Brain.* She describes pioneering experiments in the field of neuroplasticity that investigate how the brain can undergo wholesale change. These experiments reveal that the brain is capable not only of altering its structure but also of generating new neurons, even into old age.

By the act of mental repetition, and the mental replay of ideas, we create new energy grooves. Our power to create new energy grooves means we have the power to recreate, re-imagine, and re-energize any event that occurred in the physical-material world.

We stand at a crossroads with every experience in life from smelling a flower to failing an exam at school, dealing with a promotion to falling in love or coping with a major loss. How we interpret the experience determines our reality and sets up the blueprint for similar experiences in the future. Our interpretive capacity crystallizes these perceptions in a manner that either integrates or fragments us, creating harmony or dissonance. The repetition of these ideas forges self-identity and creates energy grooves and memory grooves in the brain itself.

The repetition of these themes can lead to either positive or negative self-talk. The more energy and repetition on any theme, the greater the energy grooves available for that theme. And the deeper and more pronounced the energy groove, the more likely that there will be a tendency toward similar interpretations. The late self-help author Robert Collier put it this way: "One comes to believe whatever one repeats to oneself sufficiently often, whether the statement be true or false. It comes to be the dominating thought in one's mind." It is imperative, therefore, for you to become more aware of your habitual trends of thought.

Confusion can result when you place too much emphasis on your interpretations of events, experiences and interactions. These interpretations are simply the movement of energy in chemical, biological and energy fields. They are not the true reflectors of reality. The habit of repeating ideas may help you feel solid. You may even mistake that "solidity" for who you actually are. But that is an illusion. You are more than your biology, interpretations, emotions, and habits of thought. Far more!

THE ROLE OF PSYCHOLOGY

Most self-help books are based on the premise that to achieve happiness or peace, you must better understand and master your psychological underpinnings.

But it is *only* the Limited Self that can achieve greater self-understanding through psychological approaches to self-discovery. This is a worthy endeavor, of course, for introspection, self-examination, and self-analysis are helpful tools in the process of knowing yourself. Psychology is about the journey of consciousness, addressing as well the physiological aspects and their impact on consciousness. But if the consciousness of the Limited Self becomes the only area of investigation, the discovery of a larger, spiritual Self will be sacrificed and with it, the attainment of true integration.

We all need to find the middle path. Bypassing the Limited Self in your efforts to access your spiritual self will not bring freedom and happiness anymore than the reverse. Buried or unresolved psychological issues will continue to fester if left unaddressed. The Limited Self is fertile soil for doing deep inner work. Without that work, those issues remain and will spring up as you delve more deeply into your spiritual nature. John Welwood speaks to this in his *Toward a*

Psychology of Awakening: "As awareness starts to move beyond the boundaries of the conditioned personality structure, this expansion inevitably challenges that structure, flushing out old, subconscious, reactive patterns that often emerge with a vengeance."

When these reactive patterns are flushed to the surface, psychology can be a helpful therapeutic tool. However, its value, in general, is not the territory and the analysis of the spiritual nature of man. Psychological assistance from the hands of trained professionals can give you an invaluable gift—the gift of greater knowledge and the possibility of understanding more of yourself, your journey, and the movement of your own consciousness. Yet, any lasting transformation of your human consciousness ultimately has to provide the unshakable realization that you are at your core, a spiritual being, possessing an unchangeable nature rooted in joy.

Introducing the Eternal Self

Beyond the Limited Self is another Self, constant, changeless, integrated, unbounded by physiology, unaffected by alternating psychological states, impervious to societal or cultural influences. It functions by intuition, free of interpretation and faulty self-definition.

This Eternal Self is not searching for happiness because it already exists in the state of unalterable joy intrinsic to our very being. Your drive for happiness is not simply the thrust of your desire for self-gratification or for pleasure at a biological level. Rather, it is the spiritual call to a vision of yourself that is often obscured by the seeming reality of the material world.

What if, in the search to discover who you are, you should find this expansive, radiant self underneath the layers of personality and material identifications? How would you experience it? Many of the world's spiritual traditions describe this self as the essence of Spirit, manifesting in creation through the vibratory energy of love and light. Though you may not consciously be aware of this self, it is nevertheless real and truly who you are. While you experience life as a physical being, this self remains profoundly separate, yet powerfully a part of you, immutable, unchangeable, enduring, permanent. This self is the expression of your soul nature. Here is a poem I wrote about this essential Self:

Forever More I Shall Be

*I am
I am that which is
I am that which will always be.*

*I am immutable
I am the fortress
I am beyond all destruction.*

*I am deathless
I withstand all
For I am all.*

*When the world and the universe of matter
Shall crumble, I shall remain serene!
When the sun shall fall from the heavens
My light shall light the world of worlds!*

*When I shed forevermore my forms
I shall be with form
And yet formless!*

*For I am
And forever more I shall be!*

The Higher Self is Spirit experimenting and participating in the journey of being human. If this is so, how, then, might you find greater happiness, especially if the essence of your being is already joy itself? Perhaps joy undiscovered, perhaps peace uncultivated, but nevertheless in the purest sense that eternal joy exists. If that is true, then the art of finding true happiness lies in accessing and empowering who you truly are, a spiritual being who is also living a physical-material journey. Without the journey inward, you may find that lasting happiness is always just beyond your grasp. "*The journey inward requires deep commitment to self-discovery, and steadfast patience, as the Irish saying goes, the "patience that can conquer destiny."*

> *Being is not only beyond but also deep within every form as its innermost invisible and indestructible essence. This means that it is accessible to you now as your own deepest self, your true nature....You can know it only when the mind is still. When you are present, when your attention is fully and intensely in the Now.*
>
> ECKART TOLLE

Sacred Invitations

Sacred invitations are found in all our life experiences. The infinite is calling the finite to remembrance. It is always calling you, inviting you, to become awake and aware of your true nature. The invitation is to come to know *your* Being, to experience the infinite within yourself as your immortal soul, just as you experience the finite outside yourself as limited and changing.

Life provides the journey of experiences—both positive and negative. How you mentally frame these experiences can create either an inner darkness and sense of suffering victimhood, or a tapestry of light that allows you to know yourself as a luminous light being, divinity itself reflected in matter.

Experiences alone, however, will not illumine your truth or true nature. But experiences viewed and framed from a higher perspective, from the view of life as filled with sacred invitations, that vantage point will illumine the reflective mirror of your own self-knowing. This perspective will take you toward that which is sacred and there you will behold the magnificence of who you truly are, a Being of Light. Life's sacred invitations are calling you to this divine remembrance.

SHIFTING HABITS OF CONSCIOUSNESS TO ACCEPT SACRED INVITATIONS

A paradigm shift may be needed in order for you to participate in life and your experience as sacred invitations in and of themselves. Your consciousness can make an important choice to decide how to name your potent experiences. Consider this powerful idea: Whatever your circumstances at this moment in time, that same moment is offering you a sacred invitation to expand your knowing on the pathway to experiencing your Being.

Instead of labeling your experiences "good" or "bad", you are free to choose to penetrate deeper and gaze expansively into "the more." There is a divine harmonic convergence in which every thought and action is meeting in the Now, in the past, and is preparing for the thrust into the future. The underlying flow of energy may appear to be without rhythm or rhyme or reason to your conscious mind. But the underlying flow is Spirit in motion with our habits in consciousness and our actions in the Now. You must stand firm in your resolve and commitment not to be victimized by that flow. You possess the power to choose, to mentally frame your experiences and perceptions of life. And you have the power to mentally reframe and expand your world of possibilities. Embracing choice and the capacity to reframe unleashes your power to create a new reality that better harmonizes within yourself, with others, with nature and Spirit. In order to make the shift that allows you to accept life and your experiences as sacred invitations, you will need to practice these new habits:

1. Reflect and record in writing your mental habits and self-talk.
2. Introspect and invent new patterns of thought and action.
3. Cultivate peace and stillness with meditation techniques, for interiorized consciousness will reveal your essence in meditation.
4. Utilize systematic and regular practice of affirmations.
5. Change the idea that you are powerless to the idea that your mind has enormous power and your consciousness can shift your perspectives, if not your circumstances.
6. Abandon the idea of changing the world. Instead master eliminating your own bad habits. The world can change because of that effort.
7. Destroy the idea of your aloneness in the universe. Find one other person and extend one act of kindness to them, and you will see your connectedness to the other, to life and to God.

Small shifts in consciousness open new vistas and new visions that allow us to embrace and claim our own potency. That power frees us from possibilities of victimization, and are therefore, as you will see, these paradigm shifts are critical keys to our empowerment.

But how do you create a paradigm shift? How do you create the fundamental change that can lead you to the wider view and higher perspective that allows you to see these sacred invitations?

You begin by shifting smaller paradigms in a concerted effort to exercise choice and change. You are not a victim of your old habits and circumstances. You can remain firm on the ground of anchored change by examining your thought patterns and coming to believe you are a change maker. These inspirational thoughts around such powerful potential shifts may help in that process:

- Affirmations aid in changing your mental constructs because they are aligned with spiritual truth and call you to a perception of your own spiritual nature.
- Affirmations launch you on a journey of stating and restating that you are infinitely more than you know.
- The varied focus areas of affirmations can shift specific areas of your own habitual thought patterns.
- As you affirm your noble nature, you become aware of your true nature that was once veiled in ignorance.
- As you affirm the spiritual reality of who you are and accept the view of life itself as a sacred invitation, you will no longer ask "Why me?" but rather will wonder "What, now?"

If you still struggle to make the paradigm shift in consciousness that allows you to see and accept sacred invitations, if you struggle to believe that you have the power of choice, perhaps this affirmation will be the a good one for you: "I unleash the dynamic force of the universal power of creation. I manifest creation in the form of the good, light and love."

Your destiny is to awaken to the profound knowing of who you truly are. In your steps towards that knowing, you need to accept the sacred invitation to shift those areas of your consciousness required for you to better behold your spiritual essence.

The ability to experience events and conditions in your life as sacred invitations may require a truly huge shift in your understanding of the meaning of life. This is not a minor shift. It is the paradigm shift that will lead you to a profound metaphysical understanding. We are Spirit embarking on a human journey, the quest of awakening to the Spirit in All.

You are invited to affirm and to explore the content of Sacred Invitations. This is a multi-faceted concept that essentially affirms the power of You. Beginning to glimpse the power of you should bring new dreams to dream and truths to affirm. It should also allow you to glimpse the power of affirmations and a transformative technique capable of awakening higher levels of self-knowing. Energized repetition of truth creates a vibratory energy which aligns two opposing selves (the Limited Self and the Eternal Self). Fortunately, as spiritual beings we do have an extraordinary capacity to make focused life-altering change. You are invited to claim powerful, positive change!. The benevolent universe offers each one of us a sacred invitation:

*To pursue greater self-knowing
and penetrate into the Divine force
that underlies the universe itself.*

You have the power to touch into the sun of your being. You are a container of the power of the universe itself. Cultivating the concept of Sacred Invitations awakens you to the potency of who you are. All conditions and all circumstances, at this moment in time, are inviting you to know yourself more and penetrate into the divine within. The luminous sunlight is calling you to penetrate the sun of awakening and knowing.

Self-Forgiveness

What if you feel you have failed in your thoughts and actions? What if your self-judgment is harsh and unrelenting? All humans have a moral compass because our lives are more than human. Divinity itself resides within, untouched by human misconduct and errors in living and acting. Swami Sri Yukteswar, the guru of Paramahansa Yoganada said, "Human conduct is ever unreliable until man is anchored in the Divine." The solution from this perspective is to become anchored in the Divine.

Meditation is not only a necessity – it is the pathway to penetrating the divine within. No human error is ever beyond the redemptive hand. If you cast your intention to claim the highest expression of your own nature, you shall be lifted up to claiming the highest resonance within. Interiorize your consciousness by balanced techniques of meditation, and dive into your self-discovery and divine awakening.

To claim or regain your moral compass embrace the truth and the light of who you are. The redemptive hand will lift you up in Love! Awakening and forgiveness are yours! Claim your true life and destiny!

The Sacred Invitation to Self-Forgiving and And Forgiving Others

You should also embrace the task of working on forgiveness. When you embrace the idea of forgiveness as a sacred invitation you elevate your efforts to a new level. It is only when you master forgiving another that you become free by forgiving yourself. You can then break the chains and escape the crushing jail that was created by your perception of self-blame for not escaping the harm or violation you experienced by another or others. Your liberation is at hand!

Forgiving another is the sacred invitation that frees you to forgive yourself and to love yourself. You have the choice and power to choose. Your liberation is at hand!

The Well of Silence Within

Meditation has been used through the centuries as a method for acquiring spiritual self-knowledge. It is based on the idea that as the consciousness becomes interiorized, we have more access to our essence or true nature. "Be still and know that I am God" conveys this truth with simple clarity. The silence of meditation is not just a passive quietness. It embodies a dynamic and vast consciousness far beyond our usual experience. In this mental stillness, we can access our own hidden consciousness.

Our Dual Nature: The Limited Self and the Eternal Self

Real transformation to achieve a sense of empowerment must include the cultivation of a relationship with your truest self, the Eternal Self, which rests in the center of your being. This Self begins to emerge, as we have seen, when you peel away the layers of ego consciousness through meditation, introspection and other awareness-based practices. All beings, no matter how reactionary, fearful, violent or lost, can open themselves to the sacred within and become free. Spirit is your very being. Meditation allows you access to the deeper regions of your spiritual nature, connects you with the Divine presence within, and provides a clearer vision of the truth. Scheduling time each day for meditation practice is essential not only for peace and well being and empowerment, but for experiencing your Eternal Self, the true source of lasting happiness.

Meditation, spiritualized affirmations and will-charged visualization are all powerful conduits and conveyors of truth that promote access to your highest self. The irony is that your spiritual, expansive, all-knowing self is never in pursuit of its own happiness. Its nature is already joy, peace, and bliss. In its silence, it is summoning the Limited Self into a greater alliance with itself. In the Greek myth, Narcissus falls in love with his own image reflected in a pool of water. In a spiritual interpretation, he may be seeing the truth of his own divine nature reflecting back in the still waters.

While this reflection is generally obscured, there is nevertheless a powerful drive within you not only to perceive your true image, your true Self, but to become fully one with it. You may well be reading this book because you desire the joy that is more than an extension of the happiness of the earth. Seemingly just out of reach, we tend to fall back on our belief in the tangible self of change and vacillating, unstable circumstances. You, too, may operate on the myth that this kaleidoscope of images is your true self and that if you can run fast enough, you will catch and possess yourself and achieve a state of unchanging happiness. Like the proverbial dog chasing its own tail, you may go round and round in search of something that is already within you.

True access lies in the stillness and the subtleties of the movement of Spirit. Eckart Tolle wrote: "Your innermost sense of self, of who you are, is inseparable from stillness. This I Am that is deeper than name and form." His words are an invitation to a voyage of self-discovery. They invite your activity-driven mind and sense identification to move past the pursuits of the world, toward calmness, serenity, peace, tranquility, and self-knowing beyond any definition. This is where deep meditation will take you.

For those who believe that in time they will possess happiness because of the nature of their dreams and goals, the world offers strong encouragement to continue to pursue that pathway. Nothing that another may say will alter the momentum of that journey. For those who doubt that the world in and of itself will be able to provide happiness, know that such perceptions can be reversed. Doubt can be a catalyst for us to seek deeper, thus creating a bridge to a new level of integration between the two selves.

The tools of affirmation, meditation and visualization are the bridge-builders for the fragmented parts of your Limited Self. To achieve true, lasting happiness, the self of the world must come into alliance, alignment and attunement with the Divine aspect of the self.

Characteristics of the Limited Self and Eternal Self

Limited Self	Eternal Self
Ego-driven consciousness	Spirit-based consciousness
Identifies with the body and the material world	Not subject to identification with body, senses or material pleasures
Biological and psychological identification is foundational	Spirit in man beyond all definition and identification

Our Dual Nature: The Limited Self and the Eternal Self

Limited Self	Eternal Self
Shaped by experiences and interpretations of those experiences	Immutable, absolute in being
Resides in our genetic heritage	Independent of genetic heritage
Desires to seek and possess happiness	Never in pursuit of its own happiness; continually joyful
Progresses through an innate developmental pattern of psychological and biological stages	Manifests in creation through the vibratory energy of love and light
Impacted and changed by circumstances and faulty self-definition	Not impacted by changing conditions or circumstances
Struggles with feelings of powerlessness against the Law of Change	Changeless nature is constant joy, peace, bliss
Ever changing and unstable due to circumstances, with illusion of control	Has enduring permanence, unfaltering truth, vibratory consistency with spirit
Happiness associated with fulfillment of biological drives and gratification	Happiness inherent in Being independent of external desires

The practice of energy-charged spiritualized affirmations is one of the most powerful techniques in the toolkit you can employ to integrate the two selves, an integration key to creating sustained happiness. Here are a sampling of affirmations intended to lead to that integration.

AFFIRM AND TRANSFORM:

AFFIRMATIONS TO HELP INTEGRATE YOUR DUAL NATURE

For Integration
Attuned, Aligned,
Integrated Self,
Content in Being,
Peaceful in Serenity,
Awake in Spirit.

For Joy-filled Bliss
Being in knowing
I am.
Joy-filled,
light-illuminated,
ever penetrated,
ever known.
Joy-filled bliss I am.
Joy-filled bliss I am.

For Becoming One with the Light
I am the Light
of all suns.
I possess the power
of all creations.
My name is the name
of all Light,
all suns,
all power,
and all creations.

For Seeing My Face in God
I behold the face of God.
I parted the curtains of penetration
and the face I saw
was my own.

For Becoming One with All That Is
In becoming one
with nature
I claim my
nature.
I am Spirit
in nature.

For Silent Discovery
In silence,
the seeker finds
himself.

For Intentional Focus
Intentioned focus increases my power
of concentration.
In concentration
I perceive the whole,
and the parts,
moving in perfected
harmony.

Affirm and Transform:

For Greater Purified Consciousness
Oh Lord, may I become less of myself
in ego-based consciousness
that I may become ever more one with Thee.
May I become truly a purified conduit
of Your love, of Your light, of Your grace.

For Becoming a Mirror of the Divine
May I become a perfected mirror
of the divine essence
which is You, Oh Lord.

Affirmations to Make A Paradigm Shift to Accept Sacred Invitations

For the Power of Choice
I possess the power of choice.
I unleash the dynamic force
of the universal power of creation.
I manifest creation in the form
of the good, light and love.

For General Empowerment
I am all powerful
For I receive from
The power of all.

For Perceiving The Truth of Spiritual Being
Restless mind,
Now centered in truth perception.
I perceive the truth:
I am.

For Connectedness
I am connected to all
For I am one
With the One.

For Becoming a Change Maker
I am a change maker.
I create worlds of kindness
and universes of love.
All life is changed
Because I am connected
with the Source of All.

For Experiencing the Light
I see the light of God in all
I experience the light of God within
All is in the light.

Affirmations on Forgiveness

Self Forgiveness
I forgive myself
I forgive others
I am above all harm
The Love of God
Embraces me
The Love of God
Embraces others
We are all One

AFFIRM AND TRANSFORM:

Your Love Liberated Me
Compassionate One
Your heart held me
When I felt harm
Your Love liberated me
When I felt bound
Your Love liberated me
I am free
I am free.

Forgiveness
Love envelopes me
I am saturated
In your peace
In your bliss
I forgive all transgressions
Mine and others
I forgive all
Because love envelopes me
I forgive all because
God is Love.

GREEK ISLAND

Yvonne G. Christenson

CHAPTER THREE

Power-Charging Your Affirmations

You have the innate capacity to experience joy now!
That capacity is tied to affirming from the deepest
and truest part of your own nature.
It is tied to the essence of who you are!

KEY TOPICS ADDRESSED IN THIS CHAPTER:
- How to power-charge your affirmations.
- How to create and practice spiritualized affirmations.
- How energized ideas powered by dynamic intention create fields of attraction and possibilities of manifestation.
- How developing the capacity for self-love and affirming your own lovability can be a prelude to transformation.
- How spiritualized affirmations, properly done, rewire the cognitive map of the brain, changing biochemical physiology.
- How the biochemical changes result in permanent transformation.
- How spiritualized affirmations, properly practiced and repeated, can become the soundtrack of your life.

Affirm and Transform:

How to Power Charge Your Affirmations

Once you have developed the capacity to meditate, to cultivate a daily practice, and become open to spiritual consciousness, your affirmations will become even more potent and powerful. Affirmations can be made more powerful by:

1. **Frequency** of repetition.
2. **Regularity** of repetition.
3. **Clarity in wording** of the affirmation, consistent with physical and spiritual law.
4. **Maintaining consistency** in the wording of the affirmation.
5. **Remaining relaxed physically** during affirmation practice.

When using affirmations, you will repeat the same basic idea, or content for an extended period of time. You dilute their power by continuously rewording, reworking, or changing themes. You should also strive to remain physically relaxed as you state your affirmations. This deepens access to your subconscious mind and the spiritual stream of divine consciousness. In the states of consciousness associated with falling asleep, waking, restless sleep, or states of deep relaxation, the repetition of affirmations will bring greater results. This will allow a deeper absorption into the unconscious mind and allow greater penetration and entering into the spiritual stream of consciousness.

Important Note: An affirmation should be stated in _Present Time_, as if it is currently materializing or has already manifested. A statement of future results essentially issues a command to our divine self and subconscious mind to <u>delay</u> manifestation. To indicate future benefit, or future improvement, is to order both the unconscious and the spiritual stream to cease making changes in the now. Now is all there is in reality.

For example, stating "I will soon be well" or "Positive circumstances will soon be materializing" sends a powerful message of delayed results. The Now then stagnates. Ideas expressed for fruition in the future are always restrictive and limit present change.

Spiritualized Affirmations

Few books adequately address the true power of affirmations. One exception is Paramahansa Yogananda's *Scientific Healing Affirmations*. In order for affirmations to change your life, they must be accompanied by a sincere desire to strive for greater self-knowledge. That being said, most people do not understand that they have one of the most powerful tools for change right within them. When language is infused with the repeated vibration of truth in Spirit, another level of universal power is unleashed.

As your spiritualized language affirms, your words create an energy blueprint that has the power of vibrational attraction, operating through the law of magnetism and the law of attraction. As mentioned previously, these grooves create energy channels that are deepened by repetition, allowing for a precise, highly-charged flow of energy in motion to move along existing neural highways. This then attracts similar and like vibration: "Like attracts like." Energy seeks its own level. Energy blueprints cannot evaluate the truth or falsehood of the ideas. True and false alike can be imprinted. It is the persistent application of positive thought and word over time that will allow you to shift to a greater positive magnetism in life.

> *The power of affirmations allows for a new level of alignment and integration with the fragmented parts of the Limited Self.*

Will-directed thoughts, charged with the spiritual power of intention, are catalysts for change. Words infused with spiritual truth, whether or not we believe that truth, will create energized grooves that will allow you a greater access of Spirit.

Affirm and Transform:

When you combine your affirmations, along with other positive spiritual practices including prayer and meditation and a willingness to journey into self-discovery, the result will be a dramatic increase in self-knowing. You will experience new levels of self-actualization. Powerful alignments will happen when you ally yourself first with truth and in divine intention to progress and claim your own true nature.

Not only are these wondrous events being accelerated through the practice of affirmation, but the Limited Self begins to move into closer alignment, connection, and attunement with its own higher nature, the Eternal Self. As the Limited Self begins communion with the essence of its own nature, you achieve greater access to your spiritual dimension while the ego-based consciousness becomes less dominant. That greater alignment creates the bridge over which you can journey toward true happiness. You will become a true creator of your own deliberate happiness.

> *The championing of instant gratification, supporting our expansion into the material world and its pleasures is ultimately self-defeating in our quest for happiness.*

This is not a journey of faith or belief, for within each of us is the truth of knowing our own nature. Accessing that nature is the ultimate human struggle and goal. Words spoken in truth that contain Spirit, beckon man homeward to the highest place of his self-knowing.

Other affirmations may seek material benefits, worldly possessions and greater abundance. Yet many books on affirmations rightly caution: "You need to be careful what you wish for!" You must ask yourself whether you desire alignment with your highest good. Does your desire come at the expense of others in a manner that is not harmonious with the good intention of your self or the universal flow? Will receiving what you affirm further anchor you in the Limited Self and the world of the senses? Or will you move toward the Eternal Self that is ever beckoning to you, whether you hear the call now or not?

As noted earlier, deeper journeys into introspection are necessary to achieve lasting happiness. Applying will, determination, and proper spiritual intention in affirmations may not sound appealing; but to achieve the levels of joy and contentment you seek, you must engage will, patient determination and spiritual intention. Doing so may also require you to challenge your assumptions, reframe your values and consciously contemplate aspects of your self and nature.

Individuals and the Divine Source do have the power to materialize abundance. But if affirmations are used only for greater material gain, then you may lose the opportunity for permanent, transcendent happiness. You may delay the self-knowing that brings joy.

Spiritual affirmations use words and ideas that contain spiritual truth. The vibration of God and creation resonates in sound energy throughout the universe. This spiritual truth vibrates at a different, higher vibratory rate than mundane language. When you express and resonate with the vibration of spiritual truth, the spiritual reality of your own nature is energized and your knowing is further awakened. The sound-vibration of spiritual truth resonates in the ether and words become divine embodiments of thought, a pathway to inner remembrance of your own nature. Your deeply-held desire for happiness is a summons to come to that place of joy, site of the true essence of your soul nature.

Affirmations that are spiritually-based are inherently different from those which express wants, needs, or desires in the physical-material world. A hypothesis of this book is that spiritualized affirmations will yield an entirely different level of favorable results than affirmations based primarily on desires tied to the physical-material reality.

An example of an affirmation on abundance or prosperity may be, "I have wealth and riches in my life. Wealth is mine. A new house is manifesting for me." When that affirmation is stated in this manner, the house is seen as the ultimate end and goal. *The material object is seen as the Source which provides.* The language does not express a connection to an idea, or concept of Spirit behind the manifestation, or one that includes man as a participant in that manifestation. That which finally materializes in physical manifestation must begin its journey from the realm of ideas, thoughts, and energy. There is a Source from which ideas, thoughts and energy flow.

Spirit does not follow the laws of man's perception, but expresses the reality of itself. I hope you will be mindful to have your desires reflect your highest nature and the spiritual truth that there is nothing in creation, and nothing in the realm of desire, that is separated from your journey as a spiritual being operating in a material world.

> *Nothing materializes separate from Spirit. Even if our perception fails to recognize the connection.*

Affirmations aligned with spiritual truth have an intense power to open the door of new possibilities and allow you to become a powerful creator in the universe, for that is your inherent nature. That is your destiny. These techniques, including the repetition of spiritualized affirmations, can take us to new levels of mastery and understanding. We exist as a force in creation itself. The direction of that force is best determined by the alignment and expression of your connection with one another, with nature, and with God.

The Importance of Conscious Language in Affirmations

Any affirmation that is preceded with the words, "I Am" is making a spiritual statement. "I Am" refers directly to the name of God, Who is beyond all names. "I Am the I Am" may be thought of as a name of God. When we say, "I Am" anything, we are stating that the God within us is in that circumstance or situation. The use of the words "I Am" in affirmation should be clearly stated with the proper spiritual intention. Pure spiritual intention is always harmonized with spiritual truth.

The affirmation, *"I am wealthy and prosperous"* is a very different affirmation from this one: *"Money and wealth are mine."* When there is a statement, "I Am" it is a statement of the God-aspect in man. In that expressed statement, there comes to be another level of alignment, a vibration with man in creation and man in manifestation. Instead of stating, *"A new house is manifesting for me,"* affirm: *"I am one with the Eternal Source of all creation. I am one with the abundant supply of that Divine force that is ever-creating abundance and prosperity in my life Now."* (This affirmation could be separated into two parts if desired.) When the affirmation is stated in this manner, there is recognition of the Eternal Source, the highest source of creation, the Divine Source of all life. By recognizing that Source you draw closer to alignment with It, synchronizing the vibratory energy that is within yourself and outside of yourself in creation.

> *Thoughts are things.*
> EDGAR CAYCE

You would do well not to limit your ideas of prosperity to the materialization of one or more specific items. For example, to believe that you are prosperous based on the sudden appearance of a new house limits you and improperly measures the stream of positive possibilities. You must take care not to limit the concept of prosperity from the Divine Source itself.

> *We need to be careful not to limit the concept of prosperity from the Divine Source itself.*

The Spiritual Source is the supplier of all. Affirmations that directly, or indirectly, affirm that truth will generate a greater access to the Source itself. To believe your possibilities are limited in any way, is to negate the truth of our being a receiver from the Eternal wellspring of all-giving, all-supply, and all-life. In the statement *"Money and wealth are mine,"* wealth again is seen as the source of the manifestation. Such an affirmation does not recognize the opportunity for co-creation with Spirit. The ego-identified man becomes the primary focus of manifestation, separate from Spirit, whereas properly formulated affirmations acknowledge that wealth is a direct manifestation or by-product, of that Eternal Source.

As you deepen your practice of affirmation, you may become aware of certain contrary beliefs. If you affirm greater expression of creativity, but your self-dialogue and interior thought process associate creativity with financial need, then your results will be diminished. Any thought that implies "creativity cannot generate financial success for me" minimizes the possibility of financial success through creative and artistic work. Creativity paired with the idea of lack will always, by the law of magnetic attraction, create a state of lack. Despite such a belief, you should affirm that prosperity and creativity may be powerfully paired. Over time, your affirmation will help you see that creative expression and financial success may be achieved simultaneously.

CREATIVITY: WE UNLEASH IT. WE DON'T ACQUIRE IT

Your real power is not in the acquisition of creativity, but in the unlocking and unleashing of the dormant power of the Creator within. This occurs when you open to your Divine nature. You express more creativity when you:

- Claim creativity as your birthright.
- Explore your dreams and inspirations.
- Make time for creative endeavors.
- Journal as a creative tool. (A good resource is *The Artists' Way* by Julia Cameron.)
- Become more aware/conscious of what holds you back and work on reversing those thoughts/behaviors.
- Visualize and affirm creativity.

Exploring your Dreams as Sources of Inspiration and Creativity

No dream can manifest without first allowing yourself to dream. What are your most precious dreams? What are the hopes and desires you want to experience? The dreams you dream in your waking state are the hopes and desires that you long to achieve. Explore these ideas, desires and urges.

Are you curious about new areas of creative expression? No image can take form without the imagination. No energy can move forward by sheer willpower alone. You must first have the framework for it. See yourself as a powerful creator capable of recasting old roles and manufacturing new mental movie scripts in which you are more joyous, happy, and creatively expressive.

To do this, invite imagination to a new level. Envision that you are an actor creating the script of your life on the big screen. Mentally cast yourself in a creative role. What does that part look like? Does it involve a high level of performance with a specific skill? Or do you see the actor exhibiting definite attributes? Is there a specific talent, or area of mastery you desire to explore, exhibit, or perform? Let your imagination open fully, without entertaining any limitation. What would your life look like if you were absolutely assured of success?

To increase your capacity to imagine, practice visualizing the various roles. Combining the visualization with the successful emotional feeling state will intensify the experience. Giving form to dreams, making them concrete in your imagination, and feeling the experience *as if it were real*, will further stimulate the creative process. The time to begin is Now. We must not only give ourselves permission to dream, but cast ourselves as the star performer in our personalized dream-script.

Write down your thoughts and feelings in a journal reserved for exploring your dreams. You will only be able to explore which dreams are worth pursuing, if you are fully clear about what they are. Here is an affirmation, properly stated, that will help you access and cultivate your innate creativity:

Affirm and Transform:

For Dynamic Co-creating
I am an instrument
of divine creativity.
I am a dynamic co-creator
with the universe.
Expansive, creative energy
is manifesting from me Now.

Affirmations and Self-Love: Everything You Need Lies Within

> *To express, expand, and embrace your I-ness, stretch your arms and wrap them tenderly around yourself.*

Nurturing your relationship with yourself will further energize your affirmations with force and intensity by invigorating them with the love vibration. You are most truly yourself when you learn to love, cherish and honor your own heart and the attributes that make you who you truly are. Only out of this self-love can you truly love others and transform yourself.

Most of us agree, at least theoretically, that we need to love ourselves. But do you *live that love* in your innermost thoughts, feelings and behaviors? Let's take a closer look at how you can take the concept of self-love and make it a powerful daily affirmation that permeates your life.

- When you love yourself unconditionally, you place no limits on how to behave or how to be to accept yourself.

- Self-love ignores "if-then" clauses that establish conditions for accepting and loving yourself.

- You accept and love yourself because you exist rather than for what you do.

- Empowerment begins and ends with self-love.
- Self-acceptance is an act of self-loving.
- You contain creation itself; creativity and power must exude from within. Lovingly embrace that concept of self.
- Celebrate yourself as a conveyor of light, a generator of possibilities, and a divine expression of the Infinite.
- By developing greater self-love there is a greater alignment between the Limited and Eternal Selves.

The following poem expresses the truth about your self and every human being, that you are a Gift

The Gift of You

*You are condensed starlight,
the sun and the moon of the universe.
You are a creator of divine sparks and emanations.
You are a carrier of the keys to the universe.*

*In your touch, hope awakens.
In your words, the sun shines brighter.
In your prayers, the moon softens the night.
And in your living, all the stars shine,*

*Awakened from their sleep by your desires for knowing
and because you are.*

Going Deeper: Journaling Questions

- How do you feel about the idea that the first love relationship to be cultivated is the love for yourself? Why would this be true?
- Do you see yourself as lovable, worthy, and empowered?

- Do you see loving yourself as a valid goal? Or, do you feel self-love is egotistical?
- Do you feel you deserve love and are worthy of being loved?
- If someone said, "you have a lovable nature," what comes to mind?
- Do your ideas of love revolve primarily around romance and a physical relationship?
- What emotions do you feel when you hear "love yourself"?
- Do you feel a deep sense of peace and contentment about your worth and identity? Or, do you look for validation from others?
- Have you transferred any of your power to another, or a cause, trying to get self-validation?
- Is some person or cause a higher priority than cultivating the relationship with yourself? In the name of "duty" or "role expectation," have you surrendered parts of yourself?
- Are you comfortable with yourself in silence as well as in the company of others? Are silence and stillness foreign ideas?
- Have you embraced the idea that self-love originates from a deepening understanding of your own nature?

When you journal to answer these questions, you may uncover deep, previously unrecognized beliefs and pre-conditioning. Eric Fromm in his seminal *Escape from Freedom* talks about our ability to transfer our power to people, political causes, relationships, organizations, in an effort to escape our aloneness. Any interesting discoveries?

What is Self-love?

Without self-love, there can be no empowerment and no transformation, for love emanates from the Source of all Life and Power and is at the core of your being. Self-love means seeing yourself with all your flaws, talents, strengths and failings, and knowing, deep down, that you are lovable. You are an inseparable part of the Divine Love and Intelligence in all things. True self love arises from a sacred relationship with the Infinite, from which we all come.

Self-knowing involves personal spiritual expansion in the vibration of love. Not an intellectual acquisition, self-love is the actualization of consciousness which allows you to penetrate into divine energy. Some may feel uncomfortable with this topic as it seems to imply being overly self-involved. However, self-love is not about exalting the personality or ego-based self; rather it is the state of consciousness that emanates from greater awareness of the Eternal Self. This awareness sees the oneness of all things and naturally extends to others. From this consciousness, you feel sympathy and empathy for others. Compassion for the human condition flows deeply and genuinely from the Eternal Self.

Steps Toward Self Love

Personal and spiritual empowerment cannot lead to foundational transformation unless you achieve not only greater contact with your spiritual dimension, but also master the art of liking your human self. You can begin to develop this attitude by writing down at least five things you like about yourself, and why. You can also write down things other people like about you and why. What positive feedback have you received? It is a wonderful exercise in self-affirmation to keep a list of all the qualities you genuinely "like" about yourself.

Any lack of self-love creates internal discord. If you don't really like yourself much, that negative sentiment will run beneath the sands of your life and eventually erode your efforts to claim love and happiness. Unconditional self-acceptance, with appreciation and compassion for yourself, is the foundation of empowerment. To love yourself is to love your essence, to see it as worthy of all good. So powerful is our need to love ourselves that lack of love can lead to illness. Abraham

Affirm and Transform:

> *Self-love is above all a spiritual matter. For it is only when we can actually see and feel ourselves as one of the threads in the vast human shawl, as deeply, indeed, unconditionally received by a passionately caring and beautifully ordered universe, that we can truly love ourselves. This true, felt sense of ourselves as a precious part of the universe is really the ultimate source from which we can love others.*
>
> DAPHNE ROSE KINGMAN
> *Loving Yourself: Four Steps to a Happier You*

Maslow, the renowned psychiatrist, wrote of this: "If the essential core of the person is denied or suppressed, he gets sick, sometimes in obvious ways, sometimes in subtle ways, sometimes immediately, sometimes later."

Your self-empowerment is a precious treasure intrinsically connected to the Source of all love, wisdom and divinity. To access it is to access the vibrational energy and essence of love. You cannot think or will your way there. You must attune your consciousness by greater alignment between the two selves. Then you may enter the stream of love that eventually becomes a surging reservoir of joy, peace and bliss.

As you progress on your journey of self-love, you begin to shed unnecessary psychological defenses. These defenses are no longer needed to shield the psyche or ego-based consciousness. You become more transparent, and a profound simplicity enters into your being, for no longer do you spend energy defending yourself. Self-knowledge brings freedom from the tyrannical control of ego-based needs.

In India, the sages have a saying "Ever fed, never satisfied" referring to the nature of the Limited Self and its appetite. The more you give it, the more demanding and less satisfied it becomes. All of us, in some manner, live life from the perspective of the Limited Self. In that state, knowing is always filtered through ego-based sense identification with the world. The ideal goal of the Limited Self in reference to deepening self-love is to lessen the ego-based filter and experience more of the divine interior.

Separation from Source is the basis of all experiences of fear and insufficiency. True transformation can only occur when you have cultivated your relationship with the Eternal Self resting in the center of your being. This Self will begin to emerge when you peel away layers of ego consciousness through spiritualized affirmations, along with meditation, introspection and other mindful practices such as:

1. Enhancing self-awareness by observation, introspection, and self-dialogue, as well as journaling.
2. Increasing conscious efforts to be more aware of others.
3. Praising yourself, and your efforts, more generously, lavishly, and consistently.
4. Eliminating negative self-talk by greater awareness and vibrant words of truth in affirmations.

These efforts create a bridge over which you can move from a smaller, more confined awareness toward the expansive nature of Spirit. You can gauge your progress when you begin to notice you are valuing and honoring yourself more in your thoughts, feelings and behavior. Self-observation is the key.

EMPOWERMENT, HUMILITY AND SELF-LOVE

Some people feel that "to love oneself" suggests pride and a lack of humility, even irreverence toward Spirit. True humility means to understand that God is Doer, and that you are part of that infinite actor and action. To honor that truth is to express self-love. True humility acknowledges that the small self is not the creator of all though it is tied powerfully, intricately, and magnificently to the Source of all.

AFFIRM AND TRANSFORM:

SELF-LOVE AND THE LIMITED SELF

When looking through the "lens" of the Limited Self you may view self-love with the egotistical tendencies of the smaller self. As you know, ego-based self-absorption and narcissism are not self-love. They are distortions. Self-love, tied to the Limited Self, expresses itself in the wants, needs, and desires of the ego. Such ego-based desires create a tendency to justify the means used to fulfill those desires. This type of self-focus can become exploitation, an "all's fair in love and war" mentality, with people viewed as disposable commodities.

A lack of reverence for life may also develop as the ego seeks material success, no matter the cost to others. This "business is business" mentality ignores the impact on other people's personal lives or businesses. Yet corporate enterprises do not exist independently of the human spirit. This disdain for consequences equates self-love with self-gratification.

By contrast, true self-love connects the Limited Self and the Eternal Self.

SELF-LOVE AND THE ETERNAL SELF

Self-love in reference to the Eternal Self is beyond ego-identification and individual personality. The opinions of others, as well as your own distorted self-perception, cannot alter the knowing of the Eternal Self. The Eternal Self is accessed by penetration into pure being. Techniques to interiorize consciousness, such as meditation, can allow you to more fully experience peace and awareness of your deeper dimensions. As you deepen your connection with your Eternal Self you become increasingly purified by the light and consciousness of Spirit.

No agendas underpin self-love when it radiates from the Eternal

> *Until he extends his circle of compassion to include all living things, man will not himself find peace.*
>
> ALBERT SCHWEITZER

Self. It is a love without bias, without prejudice, and without a diminished view of self or others. Such self-love is based on direct perception, clarity in knowing, and experience in being. Self-love is unconditional. It vibrates with the empathic heart of God. It validates the connection of all souls to one another. All is one! The human struggle is seen as part of a process, a journey. Judgment of self and others is modified by that awareness. Preconceptions and judgments are the territory of the Limited Self and not the Eternal Self.

Self-love from this perspective is expansive and universal in its ramifications. When your sense of self is exalted, your perception of your personal power and the worth of others are simultaneously enhanced. You cannot increase your awareness of yourself in self-love without that vibration including others. This is a significant distinction from the experience of the Limited Self, which is preoccupied primarily with itself. The Eternal Self penetrates into spiritual nature which is all-inclusive.

Experiencing the Eternal Self

You cannot grasp the nature of the Eternal Self all at once. You must begin with small steps. Your intention to become more self-aware will motivate greater self-examination. With self-examination you are better able to integrate the Limited and the Eternal Self. The goal is not the annihilation of the Limited Self. It is a re-ordering of the relationship between the Eternal Self in consciousness over the narrow perspective of the Limited Self.

As you increasingly connect with your innermost being, self-love expands, and you begin to experience peace, joy, and ultimately bliss. It is a long journey to that state of realization, but it is a journey that you can successfully complete. Your intention, well placed, takes you on that road to discovery, integration, self-knowing and self-loving in the experience of your Eternal Self.

Affirm and Transform:

The journey to experience that pure self-love requires your deepest commitment. At its heart is the search for your true nature as Spirit moving in the physical realm. You penetrate into it, not by faith alone, but by direct experience of awareness. The discovery of who you are as an eternal being awaits. You are a unique expression of divine individuality, moving through time and space. You are not separate from God, nor prideful, nor inharmonious; you are love and light moving through the fields of light. This is the highest form of Self-realization, the key to true and lasting transformation.

A Comparison of Self-love from the Perspectives of the Limited Self and the Eternal Self

Limited Self	Eternal Self
Finite perspective	Infinite perspective
Consciousness of small self	Consciousness of true Self
Driven by wants, needs and desires	Unaffected by wants, needs and desires
Energy may be restrictive and lacking	Energy is expansive love
Ownership consciousness around things and others	No ownership consciousness around things and others
Happiness is transitory and unable to be sustained over time	Joy is ever increasing. Joy becomes ever new joy.
Consciousness of separateness from Source	Consciousness of existence within

Limited Self	Eternal Self
Self knowing is subject to imagination, perception and interpretation	Self-knowing is direct perception of truth
Limited in knowing its nature	Unlimited in knowing its nature
Cognition in knowing	Cognition in being
Self-knowing is subject to change	Self-knowing is not subject to change
Limited Perception of self	Unlimited perception of Self

Why Do Affirmations "Fail"?

Sometimes people who have tried to use valid and inspiring affirmations for higher goals such as achieving greater self-love or integrating the Limited and Eternal Selves will report, usually after a limited period of time and sporadic efforts, that affirmations do not work. In such cases, the fault usually lies in the practice and attitude of the practitioner. Perhaps your suspicion that they will fail becomes part of your self-talk and thus is unconsciously affirmed, so the words operate in reverse of your desired intention. Energy follows thought and energized thought manifests materialization in kind.

Success with affirmations requires becoming aware of these patterns. Only then can you change negative themes to positive ones. Then you become a dynamic co-creator, with dynamic intention, will, imagination, and visualization to manifest your dreams into reality. Affirmations require patience, faith, concentration, proper practice, surrender and alignment with Divine Will to reach their full potential. As Paramahansa Yogananda wrote in his inspiring *Scientific Healing Affirmations*, "Words saturated with sincerity, conviction, faith, and intuition are like highly explosive vibratory bombs, which, when set off, shatter the rocks of difficulties and create the change desired." (p. 4)

How to Practice Affirmations

There are different times to practice, such as:

- Formal waking state.
- Informal waking state.
- Relaxed state.

Technique:

1. **Decide on your affirmation(s).** Look through the many variations on various themes offered to you in Chapter Five. Determine, and write down, which affirmation(s) you will be repeating. You may vary from this initial plan, but mentally place your intention on what you desire to affirm. Proceed with sincerity of purpose and certainty that the creative force will become super-charged by your acts of mental repetition and your regularity and consistency of practice.

2. **Proper posture.** You may sit in a straight-back chair, in a relaxed posture, but the spine should be erect and the chin level with the floor. The feet should remain flat on the ground.

3. **Intention of protection.** This will both enhance the practice and create a greater alignment with Spirit.

    a) Begin with an affirmation of protection, stated mentally or out loud. <u>The intention to call on the spiritual force should always precede the practice of affirmation.</u> An example of a protection affirmation is this: *"In the <u>Name</u>, through the <u>Power</u>, and by the <u>Word</u> of (name of divinity), a wall of living flame is built around and about me and I give thanks for this great protection Now."* This affirmation is from a former Franciscan monk and a direct disciple of Paramahansa Yogananda, John Laurence.

b) Visualizing white light around yourself, or another person(s), will intensify your connection to the spiritual force and energetically send forth this positive energy toward another. Visualizing white light may be accomplished by mentally tracing the idea of white light around the body, or visualizing a spherical, egg-shape pattern, making certain that the white light also is completed around both the head and the feet. It is not by your power to see or visualize white light, or see colors around another person that you bring forth a response; it is your vibrations of good intention that summon the love vibration in a manner that brings forth the energy of blessings for yourself or for another.

4. **Formal affirmation practice.** Take the list of affirmations that you have chosen and start with affirmation number two (the first one always being for protection). If possible, state the affirmation out loud. Never repeat by rote, but concentrate on the meaning, intention, and the thought expressed by the words and sentences. Restate the affirmation 4-6 times. Then decrease the volume with approximately the same number of repetitions. Continue through several stages until you are at a whisper level, and then culminate this practice of affirmations by a mental repetition, using the same approximate number of repetitions each time.

5. Then proceed to the next affirmation following with the same pattern.

Affirm and Transform:

> An excellent discussion and instruction on the practice of affirmations, as well as a list of potent spiritualized affirmations is to be found in:
>
> Scientific Healing Affirmations
> by
> Paramahansa Yogananda.
>
> This publication is available on-line through Self-Realization Fellowship at http://www.yogananda-srf.org/ and at many bookstores.

Informal Waking State Practice

You may do affirmations with a less formalized technique by simply mentally or verbally repeating the affirmations off and on throughout the day while sitting or while active. However, if you combine both the more formal technique and also utilize the informal practice, you will greatly accelerate the results.

State of Relaxation or Pre-sleep Practice

Affirmations may be effectively done prior to sleep or upon awakening from sleep. In this state, you may mentally duplicate the pattern of affirmation practice. Do each affirmation with focused concentration a number of times, simply repeating them mentally. After a series of repetitions, move from one affirmation to another, but always begin with the protection affirmation.

Note: After affirmation practice, you may want to do an affirmation concluding, "*My affirmations are producing powerful and positive results in my life now.*"

Affirmations Regarding Family of Origin

The following affirmation is recommended for individuals who have issues around negative parental energy earlier in their life: *"I give thanks for I AM a divine child of God. I am divinely loved and divinely loving. I give thanks for I am loved <u>unconditionally</u> by the Heavenly Father. I give thanks for I am loved <u>unconditionally</u> by the Divine Mother."* Repeat each sentence twice.

Please note in these affirmations the "I Am" statements. "I Am" is the name of God. When we say "I am unloved," we are stating the God force within us is in a state of being unloved. When we say "I am unlovable," we are misstating the truth of our essence. The truth is, God is the very Source of love. God resides within each individual, so nothing is outside the embrace of that Love. The ideas "I am unloved" and "I am unlovable" are, in fact, spiritual error. Love is the source which brought us all into manifestation. Love is our nature and the expression of God within us.

> *It is our inherent right and the promise of God that if we seek, so shall we find, and in finding, so we shall claim.*

This affirmation makes reference to a personified aspect of God as father figure and as mother figure. The repetition of this concept begins to defuse the themes around one's inability to access parental love. What was not achieved in childhood will never be achieved by simply replaying the themes of that childhood. More understanding may be gained about how it affected you, but the feelings of disconnection, the lack of love or support, or the emotional unavailability of a parent will not be changed by simply replaying the record of the past. As you repeat the Divine love affirmation given (above) with consistency and constancy, you begin to access another level of that energy stream, the basis of which is the unconditional love of the Divine Force. This affirmation has given great comfort and a new self-definition, along with a capacity to love and to be loved to many

Affirm and Transform:

people who, despite extensive therapy, were unable to remove father and mother issues from childhood before learning this affirmation technique. It is highly recommended for those who have unresolved parental issues, and for those interested in the voyage of discovery around integrating more of the Eternal Self.

SANTORINI GREECE

Yvonne G. Christenson

CHAPTER FOUR

AFFIRMATIONS CHANGE CONSCIOUSNESS

You are invited to employ affirmations to achieve the highest good and to attain lasting fulfillment by understanding your highest expression and your higher purpose.

> *Spiritualized, power-charged affirmations assist us in personal empowerment by transforming consciousness, eradicating negative thoughts and lessening the power of negative self-talk.*

KEY TOPICS ADDRESSED IN THIS CHAPTER:
- Increase your expertise in identifying core negative thoughts that can be largely eradicated by the application of affirmations.
- How affirmations lessen the power of negative self-talk.
- How *spiritualized affirmations* increase your personal empowerment by the power of true transformation of consciousness.
- How to create and power-charge your own spiritualized affirmations.

Energized Ideas Create Fields of Attraction

False ideas, if they are repeated and energized, take on a life of their own. Whether you know it or not, they create their own core energy to attract conditions and circumstances into your life. Unconsciously you may already be affirming negative thoughts and getting unforeseen and unwished-for results. My intention is to convey a clear understanding of how affirmations affect every aspect of life so that you may achieve the highest good and attain lasting fulfillment. Toward this aim, you must also understand that affirmations may be used in ways that are contrary to your highest expression and your higher purpose. Perhaps you are using negative self-talk as affirmations, not recognizing the power of words, or how energy clusters around stated ideas.

These negative results occur when you:

- Make circular negative statements about yourself.
- Say negative statements that limit outcomes.
- Repeat fatalistic statements about your life and circumstances.
- Project your negative anticipation of others' behaviors.

If you are uncertain about the power and validity of affirmations, then I would encourage you to identify any one negative thought or negative self-assessment that you have often repeated to yourself. When you mentally say to yourself, *"I am unworthy of being truly loved,"* or *"no matter how hard I try I will never be successful,"* or *"in the end, everything I attempt to accomplish is taken away from me,"* you are using powerful affirmations, but as a negative, devaluing judgment of yourself.

We simply don't identify such repeated negative statements as affirmations. We see them as simple thoughts and ideas, little realizing their power, or how they are charged by potent energy. If you are affirming the opposite of that which you want, you are unknowingly underestimating the tremendous creative power of your minds, and you are undermining your efforts to experience self-love, the basis of all love and self-empowerment.

Attempt to identify five negative thoughts, or statements of negative self-assessment, that you repeat with regularity. The truth is we all talk with ourselves in some form of negative self-dialogue or negative self-assessment, perhaps forgetting how powerful that language and those feeling states really are. When we sustain a negative internal dialogue, you are practicing an affirmation technique, but these ideas are, in fact, negative affirmations. Hopefully, you have not become a master of negative affirmations, which are disguised as negative self-talk. Such repeated negative affirmations, even if unconscious, operate according to the same spiritual laws. Your own ideas and energy-charged affirmations can work for you or against you, in your pursuit of happiness. Your goal is to use affirmations in a way that enhances your life and dynamically transforms you.

Do You Tend to Believe Your Own Thoughts?

Over a lifetime you may have become so used to your own thoughts, that you no longer differentiate between what is real and unreal, true and false. Your use of negative self-statements may be perceived as practical or realistic. You may think such negative statements are accurate self-evaluations. You may even perceive stated negativity as an indication of humility. *"I am a sinner, unworthy to be in the holy presence of God"* is in stark contrast to an idea such as *"I am a divine child of God, loved and loving in that divine presence."* It's clear which affirmation will allow you to embrace more of your self in a divine relationship with God.

There are those who feel that it is blasphemy to think of themselves in any terms other than a sinner, fallen from Grace. This is not to challenge how a person wishes to live a religious life, but rather

Affirm and Transform:

> *The word "discernment" will be used here to signify the power to discriminate between a perceived reality and the possibility that the perception may be illusory. Discernment is not the same as faith, for faith may be a personal creation, either mental or emotional, but discernment is a quite certain recognition of the reality or truth of something, and is acquired by the higher consciousness.*
>
> ISHA LUBICZ
> *Opening of the Way: A Practical Guide to the Wisdom of Ancient Egypt*

to suggest that affirming a divine connection of love with the Creator, may expand possibilities of a greater relationship with God and a more satisfying spiritual life.

You may be unaware that regularly-repeated negative self-statements may be a continuation and duplication of childhood themes in image and potent language. You may cloak negative ideas as being realistic perceptions about your circumstances and the realities of life. These thought patterns diminish God's possibilities for your life. You may perhaps repeat them in a manner that leaves you completely unaware that you are creating your present and future reality with these powerful, mental projections. You are limiting the definition of your self and the very expression of the essence of who you truly are. The practices you have been discovering in this book are designed to help you unlock the prison of your negative self-definitions and thus release yourself to the daylight of new possibilities.

You will not claim and harness that power until you begin to reflect upon some of the potential of that power which you possess. The great and true message is that we are capable of shifting and changing feeling states and accessing the greater good by implementating specific spiritual principles with your energized will to succeed. Energy and focus applied with regularity and sufficient repetition of affirmations, aligned with truth, have the power to destroy negative constellations of energy. Affirmations will a powerful way for you to claim that Eternal Self you have intuitively known but were unable to access. That Self may have been hidden by false delusive statements of your mind and insufficient awareness of your spiritual essence.

> *Keys of new creation through affirmation have been lovingly placed in our hands.*

Self-dialogue Provides a Clue

To create a new definition of self, to achieve different and more positive circumstances, and/or a deeper connection with God and your spiritual life, then you must affirm only that which you want to manifest.

To effectively employ affirmation techniques you must continue to gain clarity about your own thought processes and self-dialogue. What is your habitual trend of thought? Is your self-dialogue primarily negative or is it primarily positive? You may also need to explore whether you see yourself as an optimist or a pessimist, and whether you are similar in your reactions and mental constructs to those who raised you.

One way to know more about your mental processes is to observe your self-dialogue during emotional upsets or difficult trials in your life. What are the themes that tend to repeat themselves? If you feel unloved, do you tell ourself that

> *Affirmations work, not because of the belief in that which is being stated, but by the power of repetition that becomes charged with dynamic creative force.*

something must be wrong with yourself? If that is the case, refer back to the discussion on cultivating self-love in the previous chapter. Do you feel unworthy of being loved? Do you feel unworthy of success? Ask yourself if any repetitive ideas drive your self-dialogue. Some possibilities include:

- **your aloneness in the world.**
- **your inability to achieve deep, continuing connection with others.**
- **your unlovable or unloving nature.**
- **your inability to create lasting, positive change.**
- **your powerlessness over life and change.**

Repetition of ideas increases the energized force field of thought. That energy does not remain static, but is a moving life force operating through the law of similar attraction. This magnetized affirmation has great potency and the capacity to finally materialize the statement of intention. The power of dynamic energy directed by the mind is an expression of the life force. We are co-creators unfolding the cosmic force of divine manifestation; we do this with language, thought, intention, imagination, and with the power of will-directed activity.

Affirmation Technique to Destroy Core Negative Thoughts

1. Identify core negative thoughts. What are the dominant themes replayed in times of real crisis? Examining negative self-statements is a powerful tool toward unearthing dominant themes. These thought forms are then exposed to the light of day, to the light of Spirit.

2. After identifying the core negative themes or self-statements, <u>write them down</u> in a journal or notebook. This is extremely helpful in our efforts to become more aware of themes that have come out in therapy or self-help exploration, and to identify what negative self-talk still needs to be uprooted.

3. Next, <u>substitute a positive affirmation</u> which is in direct opposition to the negative self-statement you have been making. Eliminate the negative statement by replacing it with a positive

one. For example, a negative theme such as being unworthy of love ("I am unloved and unlovable") can be counteracted with a positive affirmation like *"I am divinely loved and an instrument for the Divine expression of love to others."*

4. The affirmation needs to resonate with spiritual truth to achieve its potential. The greater the resonance, the more effective it will be. The power of repetition correlates with your ability to manifest results.

Spiritual Affirmations Can Transform Consciousness

We can make our minds so like still water that beings gather about us that they may see, it may be, their own image, and so, live for a moment with a clearer, perhaps even with a fiercer life because of our quiet.

WILLIAM BUTLER YEATS, IRISH POET

Deep down we all desire the peace of still waters. But when the personality aspect of the Limited Self drives our lives, we are less centered in our soul nature or Eternal Self. Since it is neither possible nor desirable to obliterate the human experience that shapes your individuality, you certainly do not wish to eliminate the Limited Self, but rather to achieve a progressively stronger alignment, interplay, exchange, and participation with your higher soul nature. That nature is Spirit—perfect in being, absolute in truth, and joyous in existence. Consciously or unconsciously you likely have longed to find that Home again. Deep down you do desire to make your mind like still water, calm in the certainty of divine love and perfected self-knowing. In that claiming you will know fully who you are and what you are—a divine child of God who may have lost sight of the magnificent vision of yourself and others.

As noted in this and earlier chapters, an affirmation used as a spiritualized technique must contain spiritual truth in idea and in the language expressing that idea. To state, "I am a Martian from Mars. I am a bird, a cat, or a dog" will never change your nature no matter how powerful your intention or your capacity to visualize.

Similarly, you cannot state an affirmation that includes the idea "I am *not*." "I Am" will always respond to its God name. And you may be energizing false statements by the attempt to place a negative "not, don't, can't, won't" after the "I Am" statement. When you affirm *"I am love, I am light,"* you are stating the truth of your soul nature, rather than expressing an aspect of personality.

You are claiming, affirming, and properly energizing the truth of your nature in that spiritual affirmation. So your goal is to affirm in these "I am" statements only that which exists in purity and perfection as an attribute or aspect of Spirit.

If you listen, you can note how often negative statements are used in everyday language: "I am inadequate, unlovable, unsuccessful, not creative, not talented, undeserving, a sinner, a failure, loser." Those references, or similar types of judgments, are then extended to others. Such negative statements are simply not true of the Eternal Selves.

The affirmation, *"I am light, I am love"* states the essence of your nature, which exists in absolute truth. When such truth is intoned, the vibratory energy of spirit gains power to become alive, evermore, in creation. Your words call on God to reveal Himself and it is in this revelation of yourself that you will discover God.

For this reason, it is important that you continue intoning such spiritual statements of truth with willed intention and regularity. Constantly changing the words and ideas and content of affirmations does not allow for a deeper penetration from the conscious to the unconscious, and from there, into the God conscious stream.

Affirmations can help to break pernicious habits, but only if they are invested with the power of dynamic will and are phrased properly.

If someone has the habit of smoking, it's most effective to affirm oneself as free of all bad habits, avoiding any words that conjure images of the specific habit. An affirmation that visualizes the smoking behavior will strengthen the compulsive aspect of the addiction energy. In this instance, a beneficial affirmation is, *"I give thanks for I am free of all bad habits. Daily my power of dynamic will strengthens. I am powerful in the expression of my will and dynamic intention."*

Never under any circumstances visualize the habit to be broken, for by visualizing it, the habit becomes re-energized. Instead, imagine the growing power of your own dynamic will and visualize that you are completely free, have no bondage whatsoever, not even in the thoughts, mental concepts or language of the affirmation.

Affirmations Work with Precision

Affirmations are a tool that allow for the transformation of consciousness. As such, the more specific you are in your affirmation, the greater it can penetrate and uproot the cause of your difficulty. You are not on a quest for superficial change. You are proceeding on a deeply-committed course to discover who you are. It makes sense, then, to strengthen and utilize this potent technique, or any other, that will allow greater integration of the ego-based personality and the higher self.

When your consciousness begins to transform, you view the possibilities of greater power and greater opportunity within yourself. Affirmations, when properly repeated, are the intonation of God knowledge, of God's vibratory energy. They are a distillation of Spirit, manifesting as Sound, creating an awakening of consciousness, leading some day to Cosmic consciousness.

Because man tends to be ignorant of his soul, Paramahansa Yogananda writes, "human consciousness is isolated from Cosmic Consciousness. The mind of man is subject to change and limitation, but Cosmic Consciousness is free from all restrictions and is never involved in experiences of duality (death and life, disease and health, fleeting sorrow and fleeting joy)…the process of liberating human consciousness consists in training it by study, affirmations, concentration, and meditation….." (p.34 *Scientific Healing Affirmations*)

You have already begun this process of liberating human consciousness; continuing to train yourself in techniques of affirmation and meditation will turn your attention away from your mind's endless fluctuations of thought and emotion and toward the subtler and more stable vibrations of your higher self and higher consciousness.

Creating Your Own Affirmations

In Chapter Three, I explained that to be effective, each affirmation must be aligned with spiritual truth, consistent with physical and spiritual law, and clear in its wording. I also underscored the importance of frequency and regularity of repetition of the affirmation. You will remember, too, that it is absolutely necessary for each affirmation to be stated positively and to never mention any bad habit to be eradicated.

But affirmations are also more easily remembered, repeated and power-charged if the statement is in words and rhythms congenial to you as an individual. For instance, younger people may not identify with certain words and traditional uses of language. They may prefer shorter affirmations and more brisk rhythms because of their own musical taste for hip-hop or other forms of contemporary music. That is fine and as it should be. In fact, the musicality of an affirmation can be an aid to memory and to the practice of repeating the affirmation like a musical refrain. Just as a hummable tune or memorable lyric can become "stuck" in your imagination, so, too, can a congenial affirmation become a kind of soundtrack for your life. In doing so, it creates new energy grooves that will replace old themes and lead to lasting transformation.

Similarly, older people, or those brought up in a religious environment may prefer affirmations that use the more archaic vocabulary and rhythms of traditional prayer. Still others may want the content of the affirmation to reflect their belief in a certain savior, prophet, goddess or wise woman – or their reverence for all religions. The Affirmation for Protection by John Laurence, for instance, can be tailored to each person's belief system, or it can reflect a tolerance of all by including several holy sources in the phrase – "In the <u>Name</u>, through the <u>Power</u> / And by the <u>Word</u> of Jesus the Christ, Yogananda, Buddha, Mohammed, and all the Great Ones...."

Those who work with mantras and ancient icons of divinity and wisdom might wish to reformulate a mantra as an affirmation. Instead of bowing to the icon, the present tense affirmation might say "Through the love and by the power of Saraswati, my creative work flowers Now." (Saraswati is the Indian goddess of sacred and secular wisdom and the arts.) Or, "The Divine Mother loves me unconditionally: I feel her warm embrace Now."

The larger point is that affirmations will be more readily employed, memorized, spoken and repeated if the phrasing, imagery and rhythm of the words feels right for the practitioner.

Conclusion: Claim Your Self

Having read here about the what, how and why of affirmations, you are now invited to power charge your life. Whenever you are on the path to change, you can begin to recreate your patterns of thought and action with affirmations.

What stands in the way of your claiming your power? If lack of belief is the cause, then know that belief in your power without effort will prevent you from claiming the prize of your true self.

What stands in the way of your happiness? One primary cause may be your vision that your life will in some way be different if you change your circumstances and it will be if you change your circumstances when possible; yet, truly, your life will *certainly* be different if you change your consciousness, even if it looks impossible. Your habits in consciousness are the greatest deterrent to your claiming happiness and discovering the powerful depths of yourself.

Wherever you are in your life, take the power journey of self-discovery and personal claiming. If you start now with the practice of affirmations, you will discover that you are an alchemist who can change your thoughts. *You* are a creator who aligns with and empowers the divine greatness within yourself and can then merge with the creation of all life, with all that is. Such true and lasting transformation of consciousness is the key to achieving deliberate, sustained happiness.

Affirm Your Power

*You are an expression
Of the power of the universe.
You are a divine expression
of the thought of God.*

*Thought is the
Creative substance of all.
Change your thoughts;
Power charge your life.*

BOAT SCENE ON LAKE

Yvonne G. Christenson

CHAPTER FIVE

An Anthology of Spiritually-Based Affirmations

The preceding chapters presented a number of affirmations on spiritual themes, always to be repeated with dynamic will and intention. By systematically repeating truths contained in Spirit, you lay claim to your inherent power to co-create with the Divine. Energized, spiritually-based affirmations will unleash a flow of positive energy in your life.

Gathered below is a sampler of affirmations on themes of Enhancing Our Spirituality, Integrating the Dual Nature of Man, Manifestation, Abundance and Prosperity, Health and Wholeness, and Creativity. The larger edition of *Deliberate Happiness: Practical Steps To An Empowered Life* contains hundreds of affirmations on these and many more themes. I hope some of these will resonate with you as you make affirmations a part of your daily practice.

AFFIRM AND TRANSFORM:

Protection Affirmation
In the <u>Name</u>, through the <u>Power</u>
And by the <u>Word</u> of (name of divinity),
A wall of living flame is built around and about me
And I give thanks for this great protection Now.
By John Laurence
(A wall of living flame refers to the "white light" or the holy spirit.)

TO ENHANCE SPIRITUALITY

For Divine Re-parenting
I am the Heavenly Father.
I am the Divine Mother.
They reside within me
and I reside within them.

For Becoming One With The Field of Light
I am divine light,
a shining diamond essence
of God.
I move as a force,
transforming the world
into a field of light.

For Support from Source
The force of my positive intention
for self-empowerment
is supported and guided
by the Source of All.

For Self-Claiming as God's Child
I align myself with Truth.
The power of creation
resides within me.
In sound and form
I claim my truth,
I affirm my being.
I affirm
I am a divine child of God.
I am divinity incarnate.

For Happiness and Peace Within
I affirm
the manifestation of the good,
happiness, peace, harmony
and greater attunement
to the source of All.

For Potent Co-creation
I am a co-creator
with Light,
Love, and Possibilities.

For Divine Union
I am enveloped
In the bliss waves of God.

For Ascending Toward the Divine
Arrow spine
point starward
pulsating lightwaves
thrust to ascension.

AFFIRM AND TRANSFORM:

For Awakening in God
I give thanks
for I am awake in God Now.
I ride the divine breath.
I ride the sacredness
of the sound Aum.

For the Thundering Power of Om (Aum)
Buffalo, thunderous hooves
ride the crashing waves.
All one
Thunderous Om
Lightning flash
Resounding sound
Calling home
Sacred Om
Sacred Om.

For Tranquility
I am tranquil.
I am serene.
I am serenity
embodied in
human form.
I am tranquil.
I am serene.

For Direct Communication with the Divine
I give thanks
for I am in an altered state
of direct communion
and direct experience
with the Divine
and my own sacred nature.

For Divine Breath
I give thanks
for I breathe
the breath of Christ*. (*or any other name of divinity)

For Complete Integration
I give thanks
for the harmonious development
of my psychic and spiritual gifts and abilities
manifesting Now...(John Laurence)

For Receptivity to Miracles
I give thanks to God
for through divine intercession
my consciousness is increasingly receptive
to the vibration of God and Spirit.
I give thanks for miracles occurring NOW.

For Floating in Peaceful Waters
In the waters of peace,
I reflect.
In the waters of peace,
I submerge.

For Saintliness
I personify the virtues
of saints
for I walk in their
footsteps.
In striving,
I become patient.
In emulation,
I become saintly.

For Divine Grace
I raise my heart
to Thee.
It is the sacrifice
and the gift of my loving.
Bestow Thy grace
of divine acceptance.

For Peaceful Self-Knowing
I sit on the throne of serenity.
I inhale the air of peace.
The crown of knowing encircles my head.
I breathe the silence.

For Self Realization
I tread the sacred ground.
Each step moves me
to greater understanding.
Each step moves me
to greater realization.
I am realized NOW.

For Vibratory Attunement with Aum (Om)

In tune am I
with God
in vibration,
God in light,
God in sound,
for I ride the vibration
of the holy, sacred Aum.
(Amen may be used in place of "Aum.")

For God-like Perception and Wisdom

Lord God, Jehovah
You have bestowed
Thy wisdom.
You have endowed me
with perception.
By Thy grace,
I exercise that perception
to behold the One
in all.

For Coming Home to Om (Aum)

Sound of Om
call me home.
Sound of Om
call me home.

For Expansion in the Light

Streams of light
enter into the center of my mind.
My mind expands in all knowing.
My light expands in all being.

AFFIRM AND TRANSFORM:

For Wisdom-based Vision
Through wisdom-based perception,
I see.
Through discernment,
I act.
Reason, wisdom, and discernment
are mine — NOW.

For Unconditional Bliss and Love
The Divine Source
is revealing Itself to me.
It is peace, joy, and bliss.
Unconditional Love surrounds me
NOW.

For Clarity to see God
Unfolding in ever-greater clarity
is the light of God,
leading me
to the face of myself
and to the heart of God.

For Knowing Divine Destiny
I am one with my destiny
of higher knowing.
I am one with my destiny
of God knowing.

For Peace in the Cool Waters

The cool waters of peace
bathe me.
I follow the breath ripples
of my mind.
The still waters
encircle me.
Peace is my own.
The cool waters of peace
bathe me
ever more.

For Energizing in the Light

I am energized.
I exude
God's healing light.

For Union of All in the Divine

The divinity of God
is within you (or name of individual).
The divinity of God
is within me.
The divinity of God
unites us all.

AFFIRM AND TRANSFORM:

The Divinity of God in All
The divinity of God
is manifesting
within each and every soul
that I am experiencing.
My capacity to discern
the divinity of God in every soul
is increasing daily.

For Greater Purified Consciousness
Oh Lord, may I become less of myself
in ego-based consciousness
that I may become ever more one with Thee.
May I become truly a purified conduit
of Your love, of Your light, of Your grace.

AFFIRMATIONS TO INTEGRATE OUR DUAL NATURE: ETERNAL & LIMITED SELVES

For Attunement With The Divine
Attuned, Aligned,
Integrated Self.
Content in Being,
Peaceful in Serenity,
Awake in Spirit.

For Joy-filled Knowing
Being in knowing
I am.
Joy-filled,
light-illuminated,
ever penetrated,
ever known.
Joy-filled bliss I am.
Joy-filled bliss I am.

For Aligning with Essence
Celestial Light,
align me with the truth
of my essence and the
power of Spirit.

For Interior Peace in the Divine
Clear perception is mine.
Contemplative awareness
is mine.
My Interiorized Consciousness
brings me peace.

For Beholding the Face of God
I behold the face of God.
I parted the curtains of penetration
and the face I saw
was my own.

AFFIRM AND TRANSFORM:

For Self-Claiming Spirit in Nature
In becoming one
with nature
I claim my nature.
I am Spirit
in nature.

For Finding Self in Silence
In silence,
the seeker finds
himself.

For Mirroring The Divine Essence
Oh Lord, may I become less of myself
in ego-based consciousness
that I may become ever more one with Thee.
May I become truly a purified conduit
of Your love, of Your light, of Your grace.
May I become a perfected mirror
of the divine essence
which is You, Oh Lord.

For Empowerment in the Light
Radiant light
of possibilities,
I see the
inherent power
within me.
I claim the light.
I claim the possibilities.
I claim the power
of knowing myself.

For Receiving All

The eternal wellspring
of all giving,
of all creation,
and all life
bestows upon me
all giving,
all Light, and
all love.

For Attunement as a Child of God

I am a Divine Child of God.
I am awakening in God now.
Oh Lord, how may I be of service to You on this day!
Oh Lord, perfect my consciousness
that in perfect attunement and intuition
I may receive Your blessings.
The silent seeker finds.
And, in finding,
seeks no more.
I walk in
the footsteps
of all saints
and all true
prophets.
Each step aligns
me with their truth.
Each step aligns
me with the truth
of my own nature.
I walk with
true saints
and
true prophets.

Affirm and Transform:

Affirmations for Manifestation

For Harmonious Manifestation
Divine Source, Your desire
for me is manifesting.
It is harmonious
with my life purpose
and my higher self.

For the Cornucopia of Manifestation
The cornucopia
of all my desires overflows.
The bounty and the harvest
is ever greater in manifestation.
In the bounty I have discovered
my sole remaining desire
is to know Thee better.
That desire is now manifesting.

For Manifesting the Higher Good
I am attuned to the Divine will.
That which is for the higher good
is now manifesting.
In gratitude and reverence
I receive,
knowing that the bounty of love
and the bounty of God
is ever blessing me
in divine manifestation.

For Focus to Manifest

Night and day,
I am focused
in concentration.
My one-pointed focus
illumines all solutions
and dissolves all problems.
The power to create
is my birthright
manifesting.

For Fertility Like the Earth's

The soil of the earth
grounds me
in yielding solidness.
I plow the fields
of patience and perseverance.
I germinate seed ideas
that bestow the harvest of plenty.

For Grateful Receiving and Giving

The supplier of all
supplies me.
Limitless is Thy grace.
Gratefully, I receive.
Generously, I bestow.

AFFIRM AND TRANSFORM:

For The Eternal Light of Healing
That light eternal
destroys the vision
of sickness.
That light eternal
heals NOW.
(May add:)
I am healed NOW.
(or)
_____(name of other person) is healed now. (manifestation)

For Harmonious Manifestation
Divine Source, Your desire
for me is manifesting.
It is harmonious
with my life purpose
and my higher self.

AFFIRMATIONS FOR PROSPERITY AND ABUNDANCE

For Abundance Through the Divine
My Father and I are One.
All things whatsoever the Father hath
are mine. (John 16:15)
I give thanks for the
abundance and prosperity
manifesting
in my life NOW.

For Abundance
I give thanks for
I am a magnet of success.
Doors of opportunity
are opening wide for me NOW.

For Material Abundance Manifesting
I give thanks for the great material abundance
manifesting in my life now.
Prosperity is my due!
Wealth is my claim!

For Harmony and Attunement to Limitless Supply
I am in harmonious balance
With the Divine and the Universe.
That Divine Source
is materializing ever-greater abundance,
prosperity and resources in my life now.
I attune to the Divine Source
in harmonious co-creation.
I am receiving from the limitless supply
of the Divine and the Universe NOW."

For Mining Unlimited Wealth
I am a miner of wealth,
A collector of translucent jewels.
I am a dispenser of the veins of gold.
Limitless is my supply
For I access
The riches of the heavens and the earth.

AFFIRM AND TRANSFORM:

For Participating in the Flow of Love
I am a dispenser of the good.
I am a participant in the universal
flow of love.

For Abundance
I give thanks for
I am a magnet of success.
Doors of opportunity
are opening wide for me NOW.

AFFIRMATIONS FOR HEALING AND WHOLENESS

For Youthful Good Health
I am radiant, endless,
vibrant, electric energy and youth
in every cell and atom
of my being NOW.
(by John Laurence)

For Healing and Claiming
I am focusing
my intention and dynamic will
on this goal of total healing
with unbending purpose.
I am unstoppable
against any obstacle
that obstructs my power
of total healing
and total claiming.

For Healing and Wholeness
I am whole.
I am healed.
I am radiant in God's healing light.
I give thanks
for the miraculous healing of my body
NOW.

For The Eternal Light of Healing
That light eternal
destroys the vision
of sickness.
That light eternal
heals NOW.
(May add:)
I am healed NOW.
(or)
_____(name of other person) is healed now. (manifestation)

For Healing Through the Light
My flesh and body are light-filled.
My bones, blood, and organs
are revitalized
and energized.
I am a receiver of Grace.
I am healed by the light.

AFFIRM AND TRANSFORM:

For Miraculous Healing Now
I give thanks to God
for the miraculous healing
in all areas of my life:
the physical,
the mental,
the emotional,
the spiritual.
I give thanks
for the miraculous healing
in all areas of my life NOW.

For Wholeness and Health
All disease is removed
from my body NOW.
Only wholeness
and wellness
remain.
I claim my wellness NOW.

For Healing Breath
I am encircled
in the bubble of breath.
It contains my healing.
It contains my life force.
It contains my being.

For Divine Presence
I am fully present
with my divine self
in my physical form.

For Radiant Healing Energy
My physical form
is radiating
the energy of God.
My physical form
is rebalanced
by the healing
energy of God.

For Wholeness and Healing
I am fully present
in my wellness,
in my wholeness,
and in the energy field
within me.

For Healing Now in God's Light
I am healed NOW.
In gratitude
I acknowledge
I am healed NOW.
(Note above four paragraphs can be used together or apart.
<u>I am Healed</u>
I am healed.
I radiate God's
healing light.

Affirm and Transform:

For Divine Centering
I am in perfected alignment
with that Higher Self
of all knowing.
I am centered
in the light of divine healing.

For Miraculous Revitalization
I give thanks
for the miraculous healing
of my body NOW.
My body is revitalized
with the electrical flow to every cell.
The pranic force of the universe
energizes me,
heals me,
and recreates me.

For Miraculous Healing
I give thanks to God
for His miraculous healing
of my body NOW.
My body is revitalized
by the electrical flow to every cell.

For Participating in the Flow of Love
I am a dispenser of the good.
I am a participant in the universal
flow of love.

Affirmations for Creativity

For Focus to Manifest Creativity
Night and day,
I am focused
in concentration.
My one-pointed focus
illumines all solutions
and dissolves all problems.
The power to create
is my birthright
manifesting.

For Full Creativity
By the law of creation,
I am creating.
Spirit is dancing through me.

For Divine Artistry
The Divine
is the artist within me.
I am the art
of the Artist
ever manifesting.

For Creative Invention
I am creative mind.
I am inventive mind.
I access knowing.
I penetrate truth.
I am inspired
by the Infinite Thought.

AFFIRM AND TRANSFORM:

For Creative Force
I am creativity
moving like a
volcanic molten force.
I claim that power.
I claim I am one
with the source of that force.
I am imagination.
I am potent streams
of possibilities.
My power is unlocked.
I am imagination
and creativity
moving in the light

For Artistic Inspiration
I am inspired in my music (art, writing, etc.).
The power of inspiration and creativity
are manifesting
in magnificent form NOW.

For Creative Problem Solving
I am inspired by powerful,
creative solutions
in my career life
and in my personal life.

For Prosperous Creativity
I am prosperous creativity
expressing within and without.
I am prosperous creativity
Expressing within and without.

For Participating in Divine Creativity
I am the Creator
expanding
in my creative participation
in the NOW
with the divinity of God
within me
and divine manifestation
flowing without.

For Co-Creating with God's Visions
I give thanks
for I am a co-creator
of visions and new possibilities.
I am co-creating
with God's visions NOW.

For the Power to Create
The power to create
is expressing itself
through me.
Luminous possibilities
present themselves.
I capture the
thought bubbles
in my imagination.
My will-based initiative drives
the thought bubbles
into concrete manifestation.
Creativity shines,
reflecting
the luminous possibilities.

Affirm and Transform:

For Creative Power in the Light
I am the Light
of all suns.
I possess the power
of all creations.
My name is the name
of all Light,
all suns,
all power,
and all creations.

For Infinite Creative Possibilities
Abundance
and ever-new creativity
are mine NOW,
expressing with infinite possibilities.

Blessings Abound
I contemplate.
I see and penetrate
into unceasing
and unending
blessings.
I bow in gratitude
and appreciation.
I stand tall
In accepting all blessings.

Affirmations For Breaking Bad Habits

For Strength to Severe Bad Habits
The chains of bad habits
are severed and dismantled.
The power of choice remains.
I am emboldened
and strengthened
in my power
to choose courage
and even-mindedness.

For Will to Be Free
I give thanks
for I am permanently free
of all bad habits.
My power of dynamic will
is energized and strengthened.

For Freedom From Bad Habits
I give thanks for I am free of all bad habits.
Daily my power of dynamic will strengthens.
I am powerful in the expression
of my will and dynamic intention."

For Joyous Realization
In joy, I am.
In joy, I create.
In joy, I access.
The divine truth:
I am.

AFFIRM AND TRANSFORM:

For Creative Fuel
My imagination is fueled
with dynamic intention
and divine inspiration
for God is co-creating
through me
and with me.

For Creative Flow
My mind incubates the creative flow.
My mind is inspired with creative solutions.

For Creative Enlightenment
Sculptor of possibilities,
cast light
upon my golden form.
Create through me
O' Source of All.
Create with me
O 'Creator of All.

For Creative Power
The potency of creation
is resident within me.
It is erupting as a dynamic force,
fueling new visions
with new energy
and expanding itself
into dynamic change
in the universe.

For Creative Sleep
I give thanks,
for in the sleeping,
restful state
clarity comes to me
regarding my higher life purpose
and the greatest positive use
of my life energy.
I am inspired
and guided in sleep.

CAYNON SCENE

Yvonne G. Christenson

CHAPTER SIX

Thoughts for the Day: A Sampler

Your life can be enriched and empowered by adding a positive, powerful thought to your daily practice of affirmations. The following thoughts are taken from a variety of sources worldwide. Some may appeal to you. And, of course, you may discover your own thought for the day in your own memories, reading or ongoing experience.

> *As the mind and the feelings are directed inward, you begin to feel God's joy. The pleasures of the senses do not last; but the joy of God is everlasting. It is incomparable!*
> PARAMAHANSA YOGANANDA

> *A bird does not sing because it has an answer. It sings because it has a song.*
> CHINESE PROVERB

> *What is the key to untie the knot of your mind's suffering? Act great. My dear, always act great.*
> SUFI POET HAFIZ

AFFIRM AND TRANSFORM:

Life should be chiefly service. Without that ideal, the intelligence that God has given you is not reaching out toward its goal. When in service you forget the little self; you will feel the big Self of Spirit.
PARAMAHANSA YOGANANDA

Let your hopes, not your hurts, shape your future.
ROBERT H. SCHULLER

Attachment is blinding; it lends an imaginary halo of attractiveness to the object of desire.
SRI SWAMI YUKTESWAR

This is my simple religion. There is no need for temples; no need for complicated philosophy. Our own brain, our own heart is our temple; the philosophy is kindness.
HIS HOLINESS, THE DALAI LAMA

A single footstep will not make a path on the earth, so a single thought will not make a pathway in the mind. To make a deep physical path, we walk again and again. To make a deep mental path, we must think over and over the kind of thoughts we wish to dominate our lives.
HENRY DAVID THOREAU

To the mind that is still, the whole universe surrenders.
LAO TZU

Let the beauty that you love be what you do.
SUFI POET, JALAL AD-DIN MUHAMMAD RUMI

Thoughts for the Day: A Sampler

We can make our minds so like still water that beings gather about us that they may see, it may be, their own images and so live for a moment with a clearer, perhaps even with a fiercer life because of our quiet.

W. B. YEATS

The laughter of the infinite God must vibrate through your smile. Let the breeze of His love spread your smiles in the hearts of men. Their fire will be contagious.

PARAMAHANSA YOGANANDA

The fullness of joy is to behold God in everything.

JULIAN OF NORWICH

Today I will factor in uncertainty as an essential ingredient of my experience. In my willingness to accept uncertainty, solutions will spontaneously emerge out of the problem; out of the confusion and chaos will come order. The more uncertain things seem to be, the more secure I will feel, because uncertainty is my path to freedom. Through the wisdom of uncertainty, I will find my security.

DEEPAK CHOPRA

The ocean refuses no river.

VEDIC WISDOM

As rivers flow into the sea, losing their individuality, so the enlightened, no longer bound by name and form, merge with the infinite, the radiant Cosmic Being.

BRIHADARANYAKA UPANISHAD

Affirm and Transform:

Faith is a bird that feels dawn breaking and sings while it is still dark.
RABINDRANATH TAGORE

Everything you see has its roots in the unseen world. The forms may change, yet the essence remains the same. Every wonderful sight will vanish, every sweet word will fade, but do not be disheartened. The source they come from is eternal, growing, branching out giving new life and new joy. Why do you weep? The source is within you and this whole world is springing up from it.
THE SUFI POET, JALAL AD-DIN MUHAMMAD RUMI

Forget what hurt you in the past, but never forget what it taught you.
ANONYMOUS

When you sit in the silence of deep meditation, joy bubbles up from within, roused by no outer stimulus. The joy of meditation is overwhelming. Those who have not gone into the silence of true meditation do not know what real joy is.
PARAMAHANSA YOGANANDA

If you want others to be happy, practice compassion.
If you want to be happy, practice compassion.
HIS HOLINESS, THE 14TH DALAI LAMA

Blaming never helps. When you plant lettuce, if it does not grow well you don't blame the lettuce. You look into the reasons it is not doing well. ...Yet if we have problems with our friends or our family, we blame the other person.

But if we know how to take care of them, they will grow like lettuce. …No blame, no reasoning, no argument, just understanding. If you understand, and you show that you understand, you can love, and the situation will change.
　　　　　　　THICH NHAT HANH, Peace Is Every Step

Walk with those seeking truth… RUN FROM THOSE WHO THINK THEY'VE FOUND IT.
　　　　　　　DEEPAK CHOPRA

Many people excuse their own faults but judge others harshly. We should reverse this attitude by excusing others' shortcomings and by harshly examining our own.
　　　　　　　PARAMAHANSA YOGANANDA

Understand that the past cannot and will not take you down. If it didn't then, it certainly can't now.
　　　　　　　UNKNOWN

Are you jealous of the ocean's generosity?
Why would you refuse to give this joy to anyone?
Fish don't hold the sacred liquid in cups!
They swim the huge fluid freedom.
　　　　　　　RUMI

We need to find God, and he cannot be found in noise and restlessness. God is the friend of silence. See how nature— trees, flowers, grass—grow in silence. See the stars, the moon and the sun, how they move in silence…We need silence to be able to touch souls.
　　　　　　　MOTHER TERESA

AFFIRM AND TRANSFORM:

Before enlightenment: chop wood, carry water. After enlightenment: chop wood, carry water.
ZEN BUDDHIST PROVERB

You pray in your distress and in your need; would that you might pray also in the fullness of your joy and in your days of abundance.
KAHLIL GIBRAN

The way of love is not a subtle argument.
The door there is devastation.
Birds make great sky-circles of their freedom.
How do they learn it? They fall, and falling, they're given wings.
RUMI

We are what we think. All that we are arises with our thoughts. With our thoughts we make our world.
GAUTAMA BUDDHA

Sometimes, simply by sitting, the soul collects wisdom.
ZEN PROVERB

Reading about nature is fine, but if a person walks in the woods and listens carefully, he can learn more than what is in books for the trees speak with the voice of God.
GEORGE WASHINGTON CARVER

When it comes time to die, be not like those whose hearts are filled with the fear of death, so when their time comes they weep and pray for a little more time to live their lives over again in a different way. Sing your death song, and die like a hero going home.

MOHICAN CHIEF AUPUMUT, 1725

When the ocean surges don't let me just hear it. Let it splash inside my chest.

RUMI

Your vision will become clear only when you look into your heart. . .
Who looks outside, dreams.
Who looks inside, awakens.

CARL JUNG

. . .love is the perfection of consciousness. For love is the ultimate meaning of everything around us. It is not a mere sentiment; it is truth; it is the joy that is at the root of all creation. It is the while light of pure consciousness that emanates from Brahma.

RABINDRANATH TAGORE

You have to leave the city of your comfort and go into the wilderness of your intuition. What you will discover will be wonderful. What you will discover is yourself.

ALAN ALDA

Each of us is here to discover our true Self. . .that essentially we are spiritual beings who have taken manifestation in physical form, that we're not human beings that have occasional spiritual experience, that we're spiritual beings that have occasional human experiences.

DEEPAK CHOPRA

Affirm and Transform:

Follow your bliss. I say, follow your bliss and don't be afraid…and doors will open where you didn't know they were going to be. If you follow your bliss, doors will open for you that wouldn't have opened for anyone else.
JOSEPH CAMPBELL

You grow to heaven. You don't go to heaven.
EDGAR CAYCE

The Great Spirit is in all things: he is in the air we breathe. The Great Spirit is our Father, but the earth is our mother. She nourishes us; that which we put into the ground she returns to us.
BEDAGI (BIG THUNDER), WABANAKI ALGONQUIN

Live your beliefs and you can turn the world around.
HENRY DAVID THOREAU

Holding on to anything is like holding on to your breath. You will suffocate. The only way to get anything in the physical universe is by letting go of it. Let go and it will be yours forever.
DEEPAK CHOPRA

Re-examine all that you have been told. Dismiss what insults your soul.
WALT WHITMAN

Do you want to be a power in the world? Then be yourself. Be true to the highest within your soul and then allow yourself to be governed by no customs or conventionalities or arbitrary man-made rules that are not founded on principle.
RALPH WALDO EMERSON

I have learned silence from the talkative, tolerance from the intolerant and kindness from the unkind. I should not be ungrateful to those teachers.

KAHLIL GIBRAN

Be with God, if He has taken from you that which you could never have imagined losing, and He will give you that which you could never have imagined owning.

SHAYKH MUHAMMAD MUTAWALLĪ AL-SHARĀWĪ

It is important to differentiate between your needs and your wants. Your needs are few, while your wants can be limitless. In order to find freedom and bliss, minister only to your needs. Stop creating limitless wants and pursuing the will-o'-the-wisp of false happiness.

PARAMAHANSA YOGANANDA

Am I not destroying my enemies when I make friends of them?

ABRAHAM LINCOLN

If we could erase the "I's" and "mine's" from religion, politics, and economics, we should soon be free and bring heaven upon earth.

MAHATMA GANDHI

I am only one; but still I am one. I cannot do everything, but still I can do something; I will not refuse to do the something I can do.

HELEN KELLER

Affirm and Transform:

Unselfishness is the governing principle in the law of prosperity.
PARAMAHANSA YOGANANDA

Within us is a secret longing to remember the light, to step out of time in this dancing world. It's where we began and where we return.
JACK CORNFIELD

Never lose an opportunity of seeing anything that is beautiful; for beauty is God's handwriting — a wayside sacrament. Welcome it in every fair face, in every fair sky, in every fair flower, and thank God for it as a cup of blessing.
RALPH WALDO EMERSON

Lack of true knowledge is the source of all pains and sorrows.
THE YOGA SUTRAS OF PATANJALI

The first peace, which is the most important, is that which comes within the souls of people when they realize their relationship, their oneness with the universe and all its powers, and when they realize that at the center of the universe dwells the Great Spirit, and that this center is really everywhere, it is within each of us.
BLACK ELK, OGLALA SIOUX

Even after all this time
The sun never says to the earth,
"You owe Me."
Look what happens with a love like that,
It lights the whole sky.
SUFI MYSTIC POET, HAFIZ

Pride is blinding, banishing the vision of vastness possessed by greater souls. Humbleness is the open gate through which the divine flood of Mercy and Power loves to flow into receptive souls.

PARAMAHANSA YOGANANDA

Lord Krishna says to Arjuna, the reluctant warrior:
Fleeting is the reward
That men of small minds are given:
They will go to the gods they worship,
But my worshipers come to me.

The Bhagavad-Gita

The unconscious wants truth. It ceases to speak to those who want something else more than truth.

POET ADRIENNE RICH

How poor they are that have not patience;
No wound did ever heal except by degrees.

WILLIAM SHAKESPEARE

The spiritual path is always about letting go. It is never about holding on.

THE REVEREND JESSE LEE PATERSON

Your mind blocks the free flow of life by saying, "This is how things must and should be." Letting go releases you from this insistent grip, and when you let go, new forms of reality can enter.

DEEPAK CHOPRA

Affirm and Transform:

How can we live in the present moment, live right now with the people around us, helping to lessen their suffering and making their lives happier? How? The answer is we must practice mindfulness.

TICH NHAT HANH

What is it that makes it so hard sometimes to determine whither we will walk? I believe that there is a subtle magnetism in Nature, which, if we unconsciously yield to it, will direct us aright.

HENRY DAVID THOREAU

Our vision is beclouded and the pathway of our progress is obstructed until we come to know that God can and does express as Good in every person and every situation.
    The Science of Mind AUTHOR, ERNEST HOLMES

It is not because things are difficult that we do not dare; it is because we do not dare that they are difficult.

THE ANCIENT ROMAN POET SENECA